IMAGES
of Rail

KENTUCKY AND THE
ILLINOIS CENTRAL RAILROAD

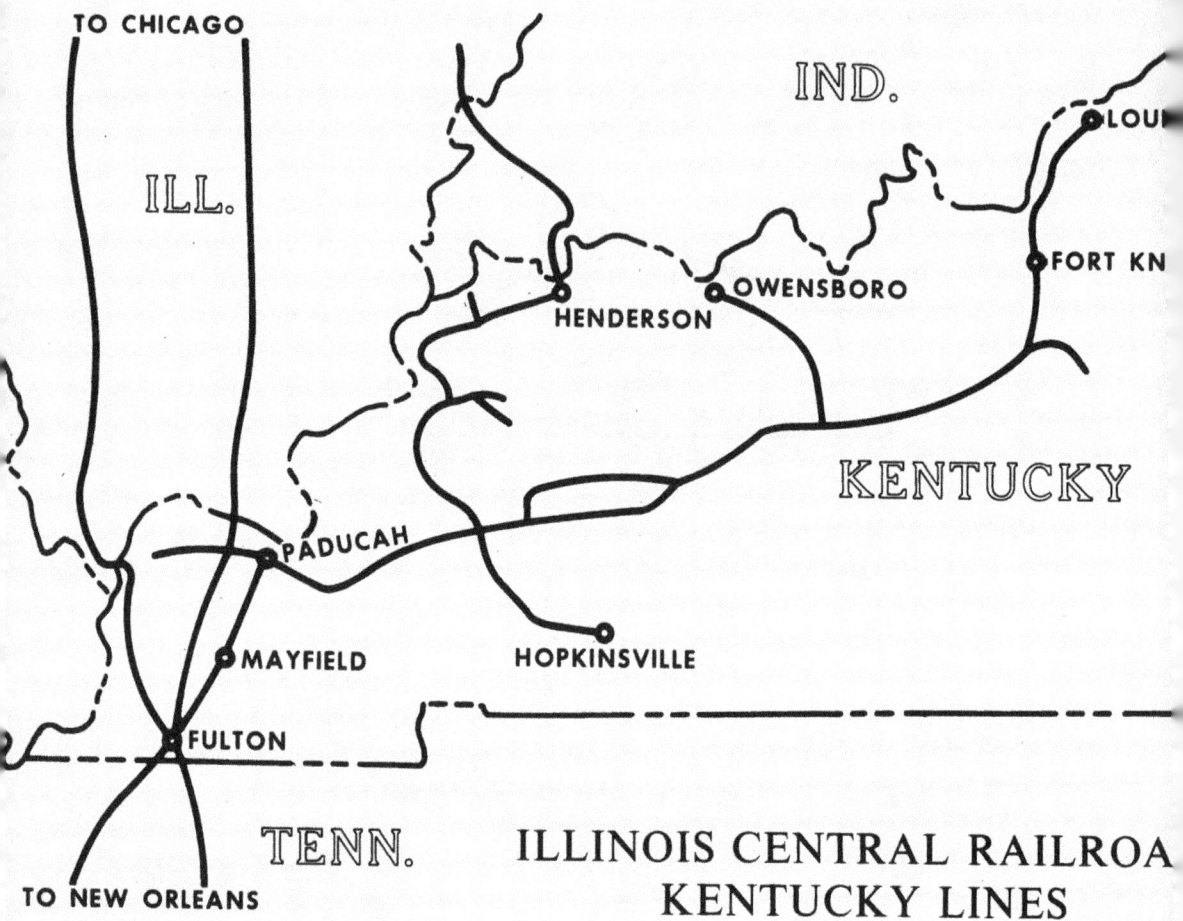

TO CHICAGO

IND.

ILL.

LOU[

FORT KN

OWENSBORO

HENDERSON

KENTUCKY

PADUCAH

MAYFIELD

HOPKINSVILLE

FULTON

TENN.

ILLINOIS CENTRAL RAILROA
KENTUCKY LINES

TO NEW ORLEANS

This map illustrates the different routes operated by the Illinois Central Railroad in Kentucky. The two busiest routes were the Fulton-Cairo, Illinois, and the Louisville-Fulton segments. Branch lines to Hickman, Hopkinsville, Henderson, Owensboro, and Hodgenville helped the Illinois Central Railroad serve numerous rural towns in the Bluegrass State. (Illinois Central Railroad.)

ON THE COVER: Photographers double-check their camera settings as Illinois Central Railroad 4-8-2 No. 2452 storms across the curving trestle on Muldraugh Hill approximately 23 miles west of Louisville. The occasion was an October 27, 1957, excursion between Louisville and Central City. (Photograph by E. G. Baker.)

IMAGES
of Rail

KENTUCKY AND THE ILLINOIS CENTRAL RAILROAD

Clifford J. Downey

ARCADIA
PUBLISHING

Published by Arcadia Publishing
Charleston, South Carolina

Library of Congress Control Number: 2009931944

For all general information contact Arcadia Publishing at:
Telephone 843-853-2070
Fax 843-853-0044
E-mail sales@arcadiapublishing.com
For customer service and orders:
Toll-Free 1-888-313-2665

Visit us on the Internet at www.arcadiapublishing.com

To the employees of the Illinois Central Railroad
who moved passengers and freight throughout the Bluegrass State

CONTENTS

ACKNOWLEDGMENTS

While working on this book, I received considerable help from many fine photographers, collectors, and historians. Bruce Meyer generously allowed the use of several photographs taken during his trips to Kentucky in the late 1950s. Meyer was a meticulous photographer who was always exploring new vantage points. For years, he sold prints from his extensive photograph collection, allowing others to experience a long lost era of railroading. Meyer, who passed away on June 29, 2006, worked briefly for the Signal Department of the Illinois Central Railroad before going to a long career with the Electro-Motive Division of General Motors, a major builder of diesel locomotives.

Mike Haper also generously allowed the use of several of his photographs taken during trips to Paducah between 1956 and 1960. During these trips, he took many fine photographs of Illinois Central Railroad steam in action, and much to my regret, I could not squeeze more into the book.

Chris Thompson and Sam Harrison both contributed several photographs from their extensive collections, including several rare ones that I could not find elsewhere. These two gentlemen also took time to review the text and captions.

Many photographs in this book were taken by the Illinois Central Railroad and were used for publicity purposes, or simply were taken to record daily activities around the railroad. Over the years, Thompson saved some of these photographs and made them available to me. They are identified in courtesy lines with (IC.).

In addition to the photographers and collectors mentioned above, there are several others that I would like to thank. Back in the early 1980s, when I first developed an interest in the Illinois Central Railroad, there were few books or magazines about the Illinois Central Railroad in print. Wallace Henderson, Chuck Hinrichs, Bob Johnston, and David Hayes patiently answered questions and helped me learn more about the railroad. The late Jerry Mart, Joe Wirth, and Lloyd Stagner also provided me with considerable information about the Illinois Central Railroad's locomotives and train operations.

Finally, I would like to extend a huge thank-you to my loving wife, Jolinne, and my ever-patient daughter, Rebecca, for their unending support.

INTRODUCTION

The Illinois Central Railroad (IC) operated approximately 550 miles of tracks throughout Kentucky. This track blanketed the western half of the state from the Mississippi River to Louisville, the state's largest city. Other major cities served by the IC included Paducah, Hopkinsville, Henderson, Madisonville, Owensboro, and Elizabethtown. The IC also served dozens of small, often-overlooked towns such as Gracey, Viola, Nortonville, and Vine Grove.

Coal mining has long played an important part in Kentucky's economy, and it was also an important part of IC's history. Until the 1970s, approximately one-third of all freight hauled by the IC was coal, but in Kentucky that figure was closer to one-half. Other major types of freight hauled by the IC in Kentucky included corn, tobacco, steel, and chemicals.

The IC was also known for its fast passenger trains, including the famed *City of New Orleans* and the all-Pullman *Panama Limited*. Both trains passed through Kentucky along with lesser-known trains, such as the *Louisiane, Creole,* and *Seminole.* Another train was the *Southern Express,* which was an express train in name only. This train took nearly 33 hours to go from Chicago to New Orleans, stopping at nearly every station along the way to deliver mail and packages.

Coal and passenger trains helped create IC's legacy in Kentucky, but it took the railroad a long time to arrive in the Bluegrass State. The IC was chartered on February 10, 1851, to build a mainline from Cairo, Illinois, north to Dunleith, Illinois. The railroad also planned to build a branch from Centralia (a newly formed town named for the railroad) north to the small but growing community of Chicago. The Cairo-Dunleith route was completed in January 1855, and the line to Chicago was completed on September 27, 1856.

After completing the charter lines the IC did not add another mile of mainline trackage until 1869, when a route across Iowa was purchased. Then, in 1876, the IC took over two southern roads, including the Mississippi Central Railroad running from East Cairo, Kentucky, (directly opposite Cairo, Illinois,) south through Fulton, Kentucky, to Canton, Mississippi. The IC also took over the New Orleans, Jackson, and Great Northern Railroad running south from Canton, Mississippi, to New Orleans. For legal reasons, the IC could not purchase the Mississippi Central Railroad and the New Orleans, Jackson, and Great Northern Railroad directly. Instead, the two railroads were purchased by a newly formed subsidiary, the Chicago, St. Louis, and New Orleans Railroad.

With these purchases, the IC had a direct route between Chicago and New Orleans, but there were problems. There was no bridge across the Ohio River at Cairo, so cars had to be ferried across the river. Also the track on the north side of the river was built to standard gauge (4 feet, 8.5 inches between rails), while the southern tracks were built using a gauge of 5 feet. A winch on the Kentucky side of the river was used to change the trucks under the cars. The problem with the track gauge was solved on July 29, 1881. On that date, an army of 5,000 workers converted all track south of the Ohio River to standard gauge.

During the late 1870s, IC's management explored the idea of building a bridge at Cairo. But high construction costs and politics conspired to delay the project for several years. Work on the bridge began in early 1887, and on October 29, 1889, the bridge formally opened. To dispel fears that the bridge would collapse under a train's weight, nine 2-6-0 Mogul locomotives coupled together made the first trip across the bridge.

When the Cairo bridge opened, the only trackage operated by IC in the state of Kentucky was between East Cairo (directly opposite Cairo, Illinois,) and Fulton, a distance of approximately 45 miles. In 1895, the IC secured another entrance into Kentucky by purchasing the Chicago, St. Louis, and Paducah Railroad (CStL&P). Despite its grandiose name, the CStL&P only ran from Marion, Illinois, south to Brookport, Illinois, on the north bank of the Ohio River from Paducah. A ferry carried cars and locomotives across the river.

At Paducah, the CStL&P interchanged with the Chesapeake, Ohio, and Southwestern Railroad (CO&SW), whose mainline stretched for approximately 390 miles from Louisville through Paducah and Fulton, and onward to Memphis, Tennessee. The CO&SW was owned by Collis P. Huntington, a wealthy entrepreneur with considerable experience in railroad construction. Back in the late 1860s, Huntington was a driving force behind the construction of the Central Pacific Railroad (CP). Together with the Union Pacific Railroad, the CP formed the nation's first transcontinental railroad. After leaving the CP, Huntington had visions of building a transcontinental railroad of his own. By the early 1890s, he had bought or built a string of railroads stretching from the East Coast to the Deep South.

Huntington became overextended financially and needed to unload some of his properties. On August 1, 1896, the IC purchased the CO&SW. A formal merger did not occur until 1897, but the IC wasted no time in upgrading its new property. New depots were built at Paducah, Nortonville, and several other cities along the line. At Paducah, the former CO&SW car and locomotive shops (built in 1884) were enlarged and upgraded, and a second mainline track was added between Cairo and Memphis.

During the early 1900s, the amount of freight hauled by the IC skyrocketed. No commodity had a greater increase than coal. Systemwide, the IC hauled a little over 1.5 million tons of coal in 1890, but by 1910, that figure had jumped to nearly 10 million tons and, by 1920, had risen to 24 million tons. Of course, not all of this traffic originated in the western Kentucky coalfields, but coal had firmly established itself as a major source of traffic on the IC. In an effort to reach even more coal mines, in 1923 and 1924, a new 42.8-mile line was built between Central City and Dawson Springs.

The boom in coal traffic created problems at Cairo, where trains were being delayed while trying to cross the single-track bridge. In June 1914, the railroad applied to the War Department for permission to rebuild the Cairo bridge as a double-track structure. That petition was rejected, but a second petition filed in May 1921 was approved. However, the plans to double track the Cairo bridge were abruptly scrapped in 1922 when the IC instead decided to build a new 169-mile line that would bypass Cairo entirely. Known as the Edgewood Cutoff, this new route was "freight only," and all passenger trains continued to run through Cairo.

Built between 1925 and 1928, the new line split away from the IC's mainline at Fulton and ran north to Metropolis, Illinois, where it used the Paducah and Illinois Railroad (P&I) bridge to cross the Ohio River. (Built between 1915 and 1917, the P&I bridge was a joint venture of the Chicago, Burlington, and Quincy Railroad and the Nashville, Chattanooga, and St. Louis Railway [NC&StL]. In 1923, the IC acquired a one-third interest in the P&I). Then the new line ran north to Edgewood, Illinois, where it rejoined the IC's mainline to Chicago.

Coal transportation on the IC changed dramatically with the completion of the Edgewood Cutoff. Most coal from the western Kentucky coalfields was destined to Midwest markets. Previously, this traffic went south from Paducah to Fulton and then north to Cairo, Illinois. After crossing the congested Cairo bridge, coal trains had to climb the rugged terrain south of Carbondale. And as they worked their way north, the slow-moving coal drags had to stay out of the way of fast passenger trains and manifest freight trains. But the low grades and minimum curvature on

8

the Edgewood Cutoff allowed coal from western Kentucky to reach the market sooner, resulting in more business for both the mines and the railroad.

As traffic boomed in the 1900s, the IC began buying large 2-10-2s for freight service and 4-8-2s for passenger service. However, these locomotives proved to be too large for many of IC's existing shops, many dating back to the 1880s. To address this problem, between 1925 and 1927, the IC constructed a new locomotive repair shop at Paducah next to the old CO&SW shop buildings. The new facility covered 110 acres, with nearly 21 acres under roof, and cost nearly $11 million.

With the completion of the Edgewood Cutoff and the new Paducah shops, the IC had some of the finest, most modern facilities of any railroad in mid-America. The future looked bright—that is, until the stock market crashed in September 1929 and the Great Depression set in. At that point, numerous coal mines scaled back their production or closed entirely. Most branch line passenger trains were cancelled, and many mainline passenger trains were temporarily discontinued, including the crack all-Pullman *Panama Limited*, the IC's premier train.

As the Depression waned, the IC was faced with another challenge. Much of the IC's locomotive fleet dated back to the early 1900s, putting the railroad at a competitive disadvantage against other railroads and highway trucks. But with memories of the Depression still fresh on their minds, IC's conservative-minded management was reluctant to spend millions of dollars on new locomotives. Instead, a decision was made to rebuild the IC's existing fleet of steam locomotives. Between 1937 and 1945, nearly every IC steamer was improved or modernized in some way at the Paducah shops.

The mid-1900s were a period of dramatic change for the IC in Kentucky. After several years of legal battles, passenger train service between Louisville and Fulton was discontinued in January 1957. Then, in early 1960, the IC finally completed the switch from steam to diesel locomotives. The new diesels were far less costly to maintain than the old steamers, but dieselization took a heavy human toll. Hundreds of shop workers and laborers were laid off throughout Kentucky.

During the 1960s, "merger fever" swept through the railroad industry. Railroads recognized they needed to merge with others in order to stay competitive with the trucking industry, as well as larger railroads. On December 27, 1967, the presidents of the IC and the Gulf, Mobile, and Ohio Railroad (GM&O) signed a formal merger agreement. The new railroad was to be called the Illinois Central Gulf Railroad. While waiting for the merger to be completed, the IC added some more trackage in Kentucky through the August 1968 purchase of the Hopkinsville-Nashville, Tennessee segment of the bankrupt Tennessee Central Railway. These 73 miles of track became part of the IC's Evansville District.

After four and one-half years of bureaucratic and legal delays, the IC-GM&O merger was finally approved, and the new Illinois Central Gulf Railroad was born on August 10, 1972. However, the merger did not turn out as expected, and large chunks of the railroad were sold or abandoned. In 1981 and 1982, the entire Owensboro District was abandoned, and the tracks were later pulled up. Then, in 1983, the 16.6 miles of track of the Mayfield District between Clayburn (just south of Mayfield) and Fulton were abandoned. The entire Evansville District also was sold or abandoned between 1981 and 1986. The 10 miles of track between Gracey and Hopkinsville were sold to the C&J Railroad, but this new railroad failed after two years. In 1981, the federal government purchased the 17 miles of track from Hopkinsville south to Edgoten (Edge of Tennessee) to serve the massive Fort Campbell army base, home to the U.S. Army's famed 101st Air Assault Division. Known as the Fort Campbell rail, this route was still in service in 2010.

Even more trackage was shed in 1986 when prominent businessmen Jim Smith and David Reed agreed to buy the Paducah-Louisville mainline plus the remaining 9.4 miles of the former East Cairo District from Paducah to Kevil, the remaining 27.3 miles of the Mayfield District, and the remaining 6 miles of the Hodgenville District from Cecilia to Elizabethtown. The new railroad, called the Paducah and Louisville Railway, began operations on August 27, 1986. Smith and Reed also agreed to buy the Paducah locomotive repair shops, which were spun off as an independent company called VMV. In November 1988, Smith and Reed sold both VMV and the Paducah and Louisville Railway to First Chicago Corporation. Each company has since been sold several times, while retaining their names.

Once these sales were completed, the only Illinois Central Gulf Railroad track left in the state of Kentucky was the Cairo District between Cairo, Illinois, and Fulton, plus the Bluford District (also known as the Edgewood Cutoff) running north from Fulton. The Illinois Central Gulf Railroad also retained its one-third interest in the P&I. After years of unsuccessfully trying to find a buyer, the railroad was spun off as an independent company. On February 29, 1988, it was renamed the Illinois Central Railroad (dropping the "Gulf"). Under new leadership, the IC shed excess locomotives and cars, and even pulled up one track along the legendary double-track mainline between Chicago and New Orleans.

Within a few short years, the IC had become one of the most profitable railroads in the industry, a fact that did not go unnoticed by other railroads. In 1994, the IC and the Kansas City Southern Railway signed a merger agreement, but the deal died a few months later. Then, on February 11, 1998, the Canadian National Railway agreed to buy the IC for $2.4 billion. The Canadian National Railway already served parts of the upper Midwest and the far Northeast through a variety of subsidiaries. After much debate, regulators in both the United States and Canada approved the deal, and on July 1, 1999, the IC was formally merged into the Canadian National Railway. Although the IC no longer exists as a separate company, many locomotives still sport their IC paint. And the Canadian National Railway continues to operate both the Cairo District and the Bluford District. Together, these serve as reminders of the rich history of the IC in Kentucky.

One

HICKMAN DISTRICT

The Illinois Central Railroad (IC) was well known for its fast passenger trains and heavy coal trains. But none of these trains were to be found on the Hickman District, an often overlooked branch line in far western Kentucky. This 51-mile-long line began at Dyersburg, Tennessee, where it connected with the IC's mainline from Fulton to Memphis, Tennessee. From Dyersburg, the branch line snaked northward through the Tennessee towns of Ridgely, Winnburg, and Tiptonville, and skirted the northwest shore of Reelfoot Lake. At milepost 41.4, the Hickman District crossed into Kentucky and terminated at Hickman on the banks of the Mississippi River.

The Hickman District was built in two segments. The Dyersburg-Tiptonville segment was built between 1904 and 1907 by the Dyersburg and Northern Railroad (D&N). In 1909, the D&N was renamed the Chicago, Memphis, and Gulf Railroad, and afterwards the track was extended to Hickman. On December 31, 1922, the IC signed a long-term lease for the CM&G.

In the early 1920s, several factories, cotton gins, and grain elevators were located along the Hickman District, and each day a freight train made a round-trip on the line. Many businesses closed during the Great Depression, causing a slow decline in traffic. By the late 1950s, trains were traveling over the Hickman District only three to four days each week. The traffic decline continued, and in 1983, the route was sold to the Hickman River City Development Council. The Tennken Railroad was contracted to operate trains and maintain the track. Traffic is far below the hectic days of the early 20th century, but the railroad provides much-needed rail service.

Prior to 1922, the Hickman District was owned by the CM&G. The CM&G's roster included two 2-6-0 and two 4-4-0s. No. 6 was a 4-4-0 constructed by Baldwin in 1911. After the IC took over the CM&G, this locomotive was renumbered IC No. 2107 and was scrapped in the late 1920s. (Author's collection.)

The same locomotive is seen at Dyersburg around 1920 with a three-car passenger train. By this date, many passenger trains serving rural areas were losing money. To discontinue a passenger train, railroads first had to file petitions with state and federal regulators. Objections from passengers and politicians often dragged out this process for months or years. (Author's collection.)

Details are sketchy, but the CM&G also owned a handful of passenger cars. A heavy cast-iron plaque on the door to car No. 3 reads, "Passengers are not allowed to stand on the platform." The platform would have been a dangerous place to be as CM&G's passenger trains rocked and rolled along the sparsely maintained trackage. (Author's collection.)

Car No. 3, at the top of this page, had a steel car body, while car No. 5 had a wooden car body. The ornate stained-glass window at the left side of the car afforded privacy for those using the restroom, while a coal-burning stove at the far end of the car provided heat. Passenger service on the Hickman District was discontinued in 1930. (Author's collection.)

The photographs on pages 14 through 16 were taken in the late 1950s during the northbound run of a local freight. At Ridgely, Tennessee, the train pauses to switch cars. The town was once home to a cotton gin, a pair of cotton seed houses, and a large warehouse. Today's train consists mostly of 40-foot boxcars and is powered by SW1 610, built in 1946. (Chris Thompson collection.)

While switching at Ridgely, Tennessee, a brakeman gives a "go ahead" hand signal to the engineer. Over the years, railroads established a set of standardized hand signals to govern train movements. The use of portable radios became widespread during the 1970s, but even today, most train crew members still use hand signals when switching cars. (Chris Thompson collection.)

After departing Ridgely, Tennessee, the train continued its northward journey. At Tiptonville, Tennessee, the train pauses to switch at the Lake County Oil Mill. The mill produced cottonseed oil from 1906 to 1971 and was a major economic force in the region. Other businesses in Tiptonville included a grain mill, a seed house, and a cotton gin. (Chris Thompson collection.)

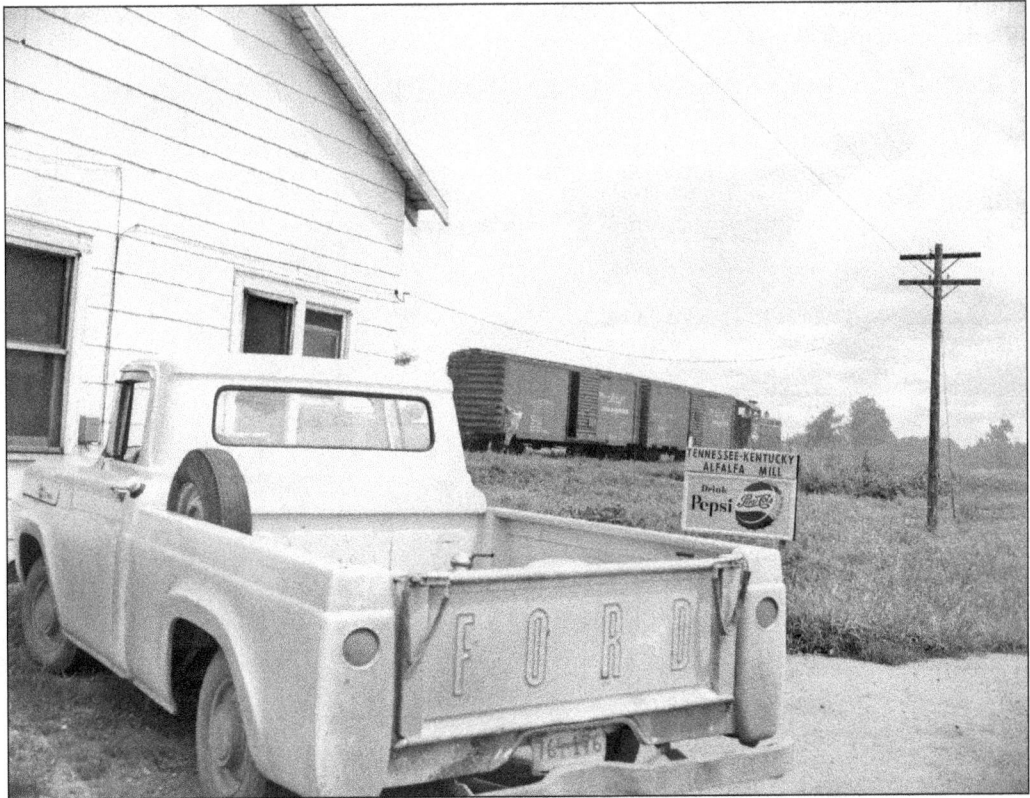

The train stops again at the tiny community of Phillippy, Tennessee, approximately 1.5 miles south of the Kentucky-Tennessee border. At Phillippy, the Tennessee-Kentucky Alfalfa Mill converted alfalfa into animal feed. The IC served dozens of small mills such as this one throughout Kentucky and across its vast system. (Chris Thompson collection.)

Caboose No. 9764 is photographed during one of the stops, with smoke pouring out of its rooftop chimney. A fire is burning inside the stove, but it is not for heat; the crew is inside cooking lunch. (Chris Thompson collection.)

With kerosene markers hanging from the rear of the caboose, the crew heads off for their next stop. Until the 1950s, the Hickman District supplied the IC with thousands of car loadings annually. But in a scene repeated all across the nation, many shippers closed, others switched to trucks, and traffic on the branch line dropped. Maintenance was cut back, and the line was ultimately deemed surplus. (Chris Thompson collection.)

Two

CAIRO, ILLINOIS-WICKLIFFE-CLINTON-FULTON

The busiest segment of the IC in Kentucky has always been the 45 miles of double-track mainline between Cairo, Illinois, and Fulton. This segment was part of the Cairo District, running from Cairo south to Jackson, Tennessee. All IC passenger trains running from Chicago south to New Orleans or Florida traveled over this line, as did most freight handled by the IC between these same cities.

At the southern end of this congested race track lie the twin cities of Fulton, Kentucky, and South Fulton, Tennessee. Tracks radiated from the cities in five different directions, all of them operated by the IC. In addition to the previously mentioned Cairo District, there was the Mayfield District running north to Paducah, plus the double-track Fulton District running south to Memphis. Additionally, there was the Bluford District, also known as the Edgewood Cutoff, running north to Bluford, Illinois.

Thanks to these rail lines, many trains passed through Fulton each day. An article in the March 1920 issue of *Illinois Central Magazine* stated that 32 passenger trains and an average of 96 freight trains passed through the city each day. That number gradually fell, but during the 1940s and 1950s, it was not uncommon for 40 to 50 trains to pass through Fulton daily.

Residents of Fulton used to call their city "the banana capital of the world." This might seem a bit odd, as no bananas are grown within 2,000 miles of the city. Instead, the title came from the trainloads of bananas that passed through Fulton each day bound from Gulf Coast ports to inland cities. All of these trains paused for servicing at an icehouse on the east side of the yard.

Many changes have taken place at Fulton. The tracks between Fulton and Mayfield have been torn up, and the line south to Jackson, Tennessee, has been sold. There are far fewer trains passing through the city, but Fulton remains a great place to photograph them.

The IC depot at North Cairo, Illinois, was well known to many west Kentucky residents. After the IC discontinued passenger train service between Louisville and Fulton in 1957, folks from far western Kentucky had to travel to either Fulton or North Cairo to catch an IC train. These two photographs capture the northbound *City of New Orleans* arriving at North Cairo on a hot, humid afternoon around 1956. According to the December 15, 1956, timetable, the northbound *City of New Orleans* departed New Orleans at 7:15 a.m., was scheduled to stop at North Cairo at 5:16 p.m., and arrived in Chicago at 11:40 p.m. The train averaged 56 miles per hour over the 921-mile journey and was one of the fastest passenger trains in the United States at the time. (Both, author's collection.)

A southbound train rolls into North Cairo, Illinois, around 1955 with E7A No. 4016 on the point. Between 1940 and 1961, the IC bought 55 E-units for passenger service. These locomotives were built by the Electro-Motive Division of General Motors, as were most diesel locomotives bought by the IC. (Author's collection.)

North Cairo was a crew change point for freight and passenger train crews. A conductor waits at the end of the platform to climb aboard as the northbound *City of New Orleans* rolls into North Cairo in 1953. On this wintry day, it appears passengers have decided to stay inside the warm depot until the train comes to a stop. (Author's collection.)

19

For passengers traveling south from Chicago, the first station in Kentucky they encountered was Wickliffe, about 9 rail miles south of Cairo, Illinois. The station was photographed one fine day in 1911 as children play. On the station platform, two baggage wagons await the arrival of the next passenger train. (IC.)

Several changes occurred to the Wickliffe depot by the time of this June 1968 photograph. Both sides of the depot have been shortened, the brick chimneys have been reworked, and the concrete platform has been removed. The baggage wagons are also gone, as passenger trains no longer stopped at Wickliffe. (Author's collection.)

Moving farther south, one arrives at Clinton, approximately 31 rail miles south of Cairo, Illinois. For decades, the city was home to several factories that shipped and received via rail. Clinton also once had trackside pens where livestock was loaded onto railcars for shipment to distant slaughterhouses. The pens are seen here in 1937, shortly before being torn down. (Author's collection.)

From the late 1800s to the early 1900s, Clinton was home to several private schools, including Marvin College, a Methodist school operating from 1884 to 1922. Many students arrived in Clinton aboard IC passenger trains. But by the time of this 1968 photograph, Clinton was a flag stop for only one train, the northbound *Mid-American*. (Photograph by W. C. Thurman.)

Fulton's history dates back to the 1820s, but the city did not really begin to grow until the arrival of the IC. This photograph was taken on April 21, 1898, at the downtown junction of the IC's Paducah-Memphis and Cairo-Jackson (Tennessee) lines. The IC depot is at right, while the Usona Hotel is partly hidden by the wooden water tank. (Sam Harrison collection.)

In 1903, a new passenger depot was built on Fourth Street, a block north of the old depot. A Railway Express Agency building was later constructed on the south side of the depot, as seen here around 1940. In the background are extra passenger cars kept on hand to handle traffic surges or to replace cars with mechanical problems. (Sam Harrison collection.)

After the new depot at Fourth Street was completed, the old one was demolished, and a new two-story office building was constructed on the site, pictured in May 1913. The track to the left leads to the new depot, while the track at far right leads to Mayfield. (Sam Harrison collection.)

·FULTON· KY· 1911·

Over the years, several coaling towers were constructed at Fulton. This particular wooden tower was built around 1900 north of town along the double-track Cairo District. Loaded hoppers of coal were shoved up a long ramp on the other side of the tower, and the coal was dumped into large wooden bins. Coal was then loaded into locomotives via chutes on the side of the wooden building. (IC.)

By 1919, the hulking coaling tower seen on the opposite page was replaced by a smaller coaling tower. Coal was dumped into a bin at the base of the new tower and then lifted by an elevator to the top, where it was dumped into a large hopper. This structure was typical of the coaling towers used by the IC and many other railroads during the mid-1900s. (IC.)

In 1929, a new steel coaling tower was built north of Fulton on the Cairo District, replacing the wooden tower seen at the top of this page. Initially this coaling tower had just one bin. This photograph was taken in 1949 during the addition of a second bin. Both bins could hold 300 tons of coal. (Author's collection.)

24

In April 1950, a northbound freight pulled by a 2-8-2 rolls toward the mainline coaling tower. The milepost to the right serves two purposes. First, it indicates the mileage from Chicago (in this case, 405). Secondly, the "c" indicates the milepost is in the Cairo District. Each operating district had its own abbreviation, useful in identifying a specific milepost, signal, or bridge. (Author's collection.)

In addition to the mainline coaling tower, Fulton also had a steel coaling tower next to the roundhouse capable of holding 75 tons of coal. In 1952, a pair of 2400-class 4-8-2s await their next call to action. During the steam era, most of the IC's priority passenger trains were powered by 2400-class locomotives. (Author's collection.)

Since the late 1800s, the IC played a key role in the movement of bananas to cities throughout the United States. The process started when ocean vessels loaded with the delicate fruit arrived at Gulf Coast ports, such as New Orleans and Gulfport, Mississippi. Here the *Musa*, owned by the United Fruit Company, ties up at New Orleans in the early 1950s. (Hedrich-Blessing photograph.)

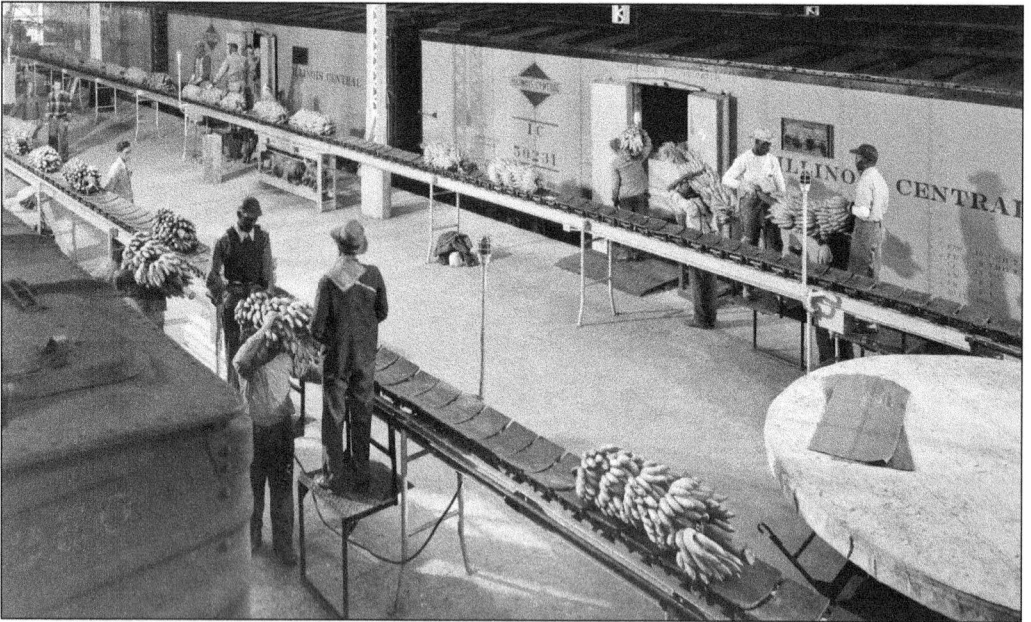

After being unloaded from ships, the bananas were immediately reloaded onto wooden refrigerated cars called reefers. These cars were cooled by giant blocks of ice loaded into rooftop hatches. Workers are seen loading stems of bananas into reefers at IC's Thalia Street wharf in New Orleans about 1955. (Hedrich-Blessing photograph).

26

The loaded reefers were then assembled into dedicated trains and dispatched northward to Chicago, St. Louis, and other Midwest cities. The main servicing station for these banana trains was Fulton, located roughly halfway between New Orleans and Chicago. In 1949, a new icing station was built on the east side of the Fulton yard across from the yard office. Inside the nondescript concrete block building (above), 300-pound blocks of ice were formed. The massive blocks were then stored inside a giant freezer (below), where the temperature was kept at well below zero. (Both, author's collection.)

Once a banana train arrived, blocks of ice moved via a conveyor to an elevated wooden platform approximately 1,500 feet long. The ice was then broken into smaller chunks and loaded into rooftop hatches. Part of the conveyor system is visible in the above photograph, while the photograph below shows part of the wooden platform. Incidentally, the train visible to the right in both photographs is not for bananas but was a manifest freight. The icing station was not built by the IC but instead was a joint venture by the United Fruit Company and the Standard Fruit Company. Not all trains were iced at Fulton. During cold weather, small charcoal-burning heaters were often placed in the cars to keep the delicate fruit from freezing. (Both, author's collection.)

Fulton's role in the banana trade did not go unnoticed by local residents, who dubbed their city "the banana capital of the world." With local businessman Nathan Wade playing a key role, in 1963, the city hosted the International Banana Festival. Festivities included a parade, a street fair, and displays of Central America cultural items. The event was so successful that it became an annual event. The photographs on pages 29 and 30 were taken during the 1964 festival. In the photograph above, the American Legion parade float, fashioned after a steam locomotive, is rolling down Lake Street. One of the more popular parade floats carried the "world's largest banana pudding," seen in the photograph below. This delicacy was typically accompanied by a pageant queen. (Both, Chris Thompson collection.)

The 1964 festival also featured an appearance by Miss America Vonda Van Dyke. Following the parade, Van Dyke helped serve the "world's largest banana pudding" to the crowd attending the festival. (Chris Thompson collection.)

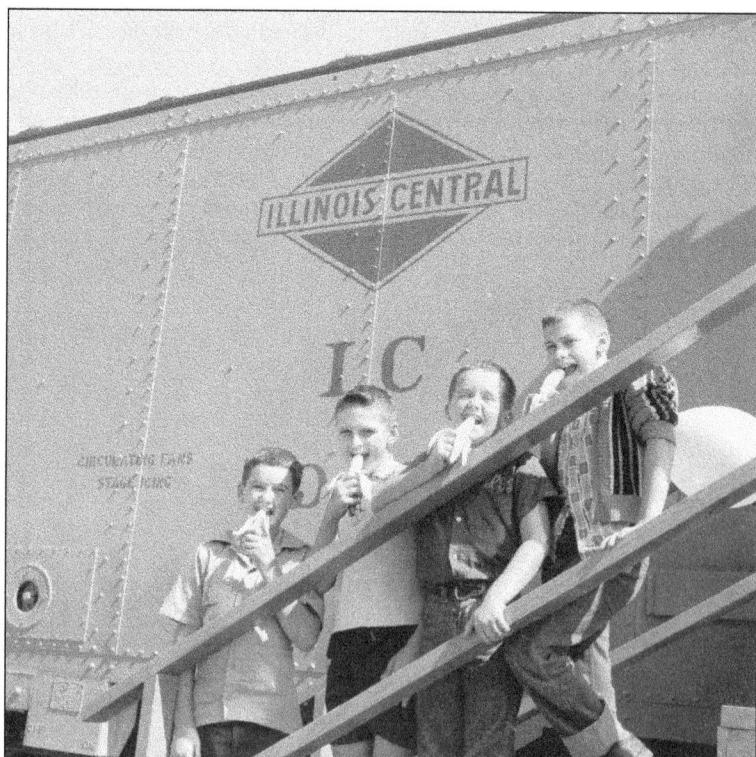

The IC also participated in the International Banana Festival. These young boys are enjoying free bananas at the depot, where the railroad had a locomotive, a Pullman sleeper, and a reefer on display. Alas, by the early 1970s, trucks had taken over the role of hauling bananas. Finding enough bananas for the festival also became difficult, and the last International Banana Festival was held in 1992. (Chris Thompson collection.)

On April 27, 1947, the IC inaugurated the *City of New Orleans* between Chicago and New Orleans. Seen here later that summer, the northbound *City of New Orleans* (right) rolls out of Fulton as an unidentified southbound train charges past the depot. (Author's collection.)

The IC initially operated a train between Louisville and Fulton that connected with the *City of New Orleans*. Initially powered by a single E7A diesel, within a few months, the diesel was replaced by 4-6-2 No. 1146, streamlined specifically for the Louisville connection. No. 1146 was photographed at Fulton on May 5, 1948. The connecting service was discontinued on January 15, 1950. (Author's collection.)

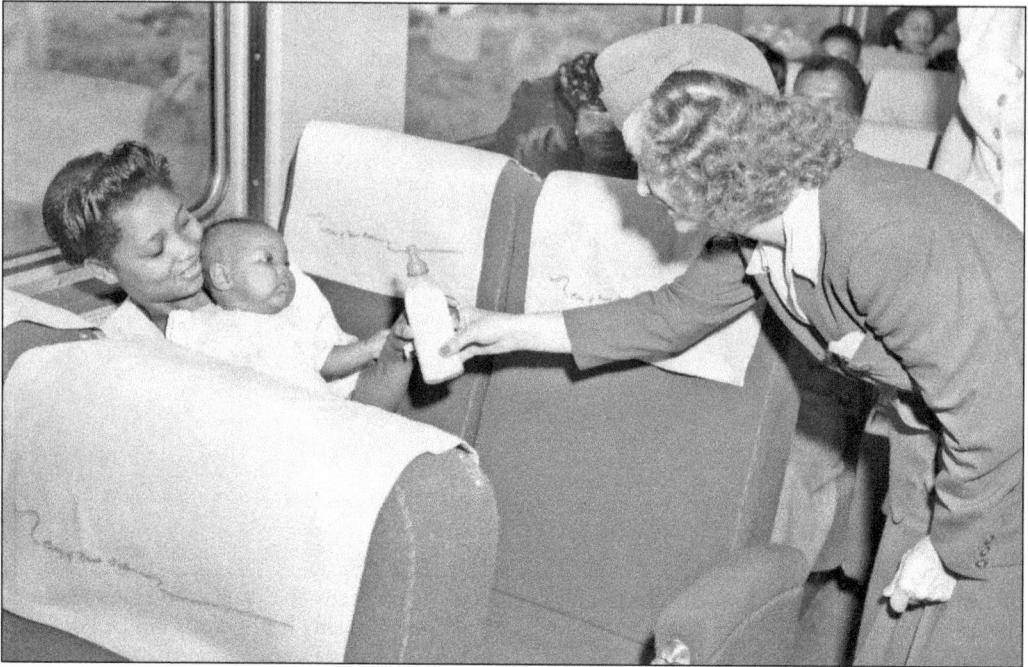

Passengers aboard the *City of New Orleans* were served not only by porters and waiters, but also by a stewardess who gave special assistance to the elderly, disabled, and mothers with young children. Each stewardess was a registered nurse capable of rendering medical care. But most passenger contact was more mundane. Helen Romanak is seen here around 1950 handing a freshly warmed bottle to a hungry infant. (Chris Thompson collection.)

For years, the Fulton depot was the focal point of the downtown district. But when photographed in April 1974, the depot was little more than a ramshackle wooden building. The structure was demolished in 1979, and today the site is occupied by a milk processing plant. Fulton is served by Amtrak, but passengers catch the train at a small trailer north of town. (Photograph by Frank Ardrey Jr., author's collection.)

On a crisp winter day in the early 1950s, a northbound freight train rolls underneath the U.S. Route 45 bridge at the north end of the Fulton yard. Leading the train is 4-8-2 No. 2521. The 2500-class locomotives were built at Paducah between 1937 and 1942 using the boilers of old 2-10-2s mated to new frames and cylinders. (Author's collection.)

A track worker is almost totally exposed to the elements as he rolls through Fulton on his motorized speeder one day in 1952. The speeder is headed north on the Mayfield District and in a few seconds will cross into the Cairo District. A portion of the Usona Hotel is visible to the right, while the Fulton depot is out of view to the left. (Sam Harrison collection.)

In June 1912, the IC established a plant at Fulton to make concrete fence posts and concrete slabs used to construct trestles and overpasses. The plant could produce 125,000 fence posts and 1,500 slabs yearly. This undated photograph shows a group of fence posts awaiting shipment. (Sam Harrison collection.)

The photographic journey for this chapter concludes at Rives, Tennessee, about 13 miles south of Fulton on the track heading toward Memphis. At Rives, the IC interchanged with the Gulf, Mobile and Ohio Railroad (GM&O) mainline from Jackson, Tennessee, to St. Louis. IC's depot is pictured on the left on December 21, 1896, with a massive wooden water tank at right. (IC.)

Three

PADUCAH

Paducah was not the largest city in Kentucky served by the IC, but it was by far the most important. IC's main locomotive repair shops were located in Paducah, along with the headquarters of the busy Kentucky Division. Additionally, Paducah was home to one of the three hospitals operated by the IC.

For many decades, the IC was the biggest employer in Paducah. More than 1,000 men worked at the shops, and hundreds more worked as train crews, clerks, dispatchers, and track workers. Employment at Paducah plummeted in the late 1950s as the IC switched from steam locomotives to diesel locomotives, which required less maintenance.

In early 1986, local businessmen Jim Smith and David Reed agreed to buy the Paducah shops plus the IC's mainline from Paducah to Louisville and the branch lines to Mayfield and Kevil. The shops were renamed VMV, while the new railroad was appropriately named the Paducah and Louisville Railway. Both the shops and the railroad have been resold several times, but their names remain unchanged.

The IC first entered Paducah through the 1895 purchase of the Chicago, St. Louis, and Paducah Railroad. This line ran from Marion, Illinois, south through Metropolis to Brookport, Illinois, on the banks of the Ohio River directly opposite Paducah. Ferries were used to carry both passengers and freight cars across the river. One of the best-known ferries was the W. B. Duncan, photographed about 1905. (Sam Harrison collection.)

This real-photo postcard, postmarked on July 15, 1911, features the tiny depot at Brookport, Illinois. At the time, the small town was bustling with activity, but in 1918, ferry service was abandoned, and train traffic into Brookport fell dramatically. (Author's collection.)

In 1907, the wooden coaling tower at the Paducah shops burned, and the following year it was replaced by the structure seen here, also built of wood. This wooden structure remained in use until the 1940s when it was replaced by an all-steel tower. (Both, IC.)

The first roundhouse in Paducah was an eight-stall structure built in 1869 by the Paducah and Gulf Railroad (P&G). In 1884, the Chesapeake, Ohio, and Southwestern Railroad (CO&SW) built a new 10-stall roundhouse, but the old P&G roundhouse was not razed until 1899. Then, in 1918, the old CO&SW roundhouse was replaced by a new 36-stall roundhouse. The 4-6-0 No. 2003 poses at the new roundhouse on December 11, 1918. (IC.)

Construction of new locomotive repair shops was well underway, as seen on May 5, 1926. A portion of the 3,000-foot-long concrete culvert to carry wastewater is visible at left. Work on the storeroom is ongoing to the right. (Sam Harrison collection.)

On August 15, 1926, crews began erecting two 265-foot-tall smokestacks at the new powerhouse. The stacks were sandwiched between the car repair shed and the machine shop of the old facility. (Sam Harrison collection.)

The steel framework of the powerhouse was quickly taking shape when photographed below on March 17, 1927. Measuring 150-by-110 feet, more than 427,000 bricks were used during its construction. When first built, the powerhouse generated steam and compressed air. Electricity, however, was purchased from the local utility. That changed in 1941 with the installation of a steam-driven electrical turbine. (IC.)

Paducah, Ky. Shop Facilities, Power House Looking East

The new Paducah shops were officially declared open on September 1, 1927. Over the next several weeks, workers gradually moved into the new buildings, and the old shops were abandoned. On November 11, 1927, the new tank shop was nearly filled to capacity. The same building housed the tank shop and the paint shop. (Author's collection.)

Only two years after the new Paducah shops opened, the nation was plunged into the Great Depression. Like all railroads, the IC was hit hard. Thousands of employees were laid off, and hundreds of locomotives were scrapped or put into storage. Seen here, a long line of 2-8-2s sit behind the Paducah shops on October 30, 1932, awaiting their return to service. (Sam Harrison collection.)

The Great Depression did not derail plans for the Century of Progress Exposition, held in Chicago during 1933 and 1934. The exposition was held along the Lake Michigan waterfront on land adjacent to IC's trackage. For display at the fair, the Paducah shops took 4-8-2 No. 2411 and dolled it up in the special scheme seen here. (Sam Harrison collection.)

Although located nearly a mile from the river, the Paducah shops were not immune from the historic Ohio River flood that inundated the city in January and February 1937. At the height of the flood, the water at the shops was 6 feet deep. The shops are in the center of this aerial photograph, while the swollen Ohio River can be seen in the distance. (IC.)

The IC took over the Vicksburg, Shreveport, and Pacific Railroad (VS&P) in 1926. VS&P's roster included two 4-6-2s that were renumbered IC numbers 994 and 995. No. 995 poses at Paducah in 1943. The next year, No. 995 was rebuilt with larger cylinders and was renumbered 1001. The locomotive was sold for scrap in March 1954. (Photograph by C. W. Witbeck, author's collection.)

During World War II, the IC was desperate for more locomotives to haul its freight trains. As a partial solution to this problem, eleven 2400-class 4-8-2s built for passenger service were rebuilt to haul freight. Numbered 2300 to 2307 and 2350 to 2352, these rebuilt locomotives received new boilers. The sleek appearance of No. 2301 gives little clue that the locomotive was capable of hustling heavy trains at high speeds. (Author's collection.)

In 1926 and 1927, the IC bought fifty-one 2-8-4s from the Lima Locomotive Works. The locomotives did not meet expectations, and plans were drafted to rebuild them at Paducah. In May 1937, the boiler from No. 7038 was mated to a new frame to create 4-6-4 No. 1. (Author's collection.)

No. 1 also failed to perform as expected, and no more conversions were done. The remaining 2-8-4s were later rebuilt at Paducah between 1939 and 1943 but with no major modifications. As for No. 1, it was renumbered 2499 in 1945 and scrapped around 1950. (Bruce R. Meyer collection.)

This aerial photograph, taken around 1940, shows the layout of the Paducah shops. The 36-stall roundhouse, constructed in 1918, is to the left, while the shop buildings are at center. Kentucky Avenue borders the front of the shop complex, while Sixteenth Street runs along the west boundary. The 265-foot-tall smokestacks were perhaps the tallest structures (excluding radio antennas) ever built in Paducah. (Kaufmann and Fabry Company.)

Steam locomotives required frequent stops to replenish the water supply in their tenders. To reduce the number of water stops, the IC utilized auxiliary tenders, which carried only water and were coupled behind the locomotive's tender. During the 1940s, the Paducah shops built more than 100 of these cars, including cars A-502 and A-503, photographed in 1941. Both cars carried 12,000 gallons of water. (Chris Thompson collection.)

Traffic on the IC zoomed skyward after the United States entered World War II. To keep the trains moving, in 1942, the Paducah shops began building 20 new 2600-class 4-8-2s. The construction process was documented by company photographers and a local studio. Construction began with drilling rivet holes in boiler plates ranging from $7/8$ of an inch to 1 inch in thickness. (Sacra Studio photograph, Michelle Craig collection.)

Next the boiler plates were rolled into shape in a giant bending press. The rolled sections, called courses, were rarely straight. Instead, depending on the particular boiler being constructed, the diameter at one end of the boiler course could be as much as 10 inches wider than at the other end. (Sacra Studio photograph, Michelle Craig collection.)

In the center of the boiler shop is a bay that sticks above the surrounding roofline. Here boiler courses were lifted vertically and riveted to each other using a custom-built riveter. The same machine was also used to rivet the boiler to the firebox. The boiler and firebox were held in a vertical position using a crane capable of lifting 75 tons. (IC.)

Below, the completed boiler for locomotive No. 2608 is seen resting on a cradle, while the firebox is lowered into position. Next the two sections will be tack riveted on the shop floor. Then the boiler/firebox assembly will be lifted vertically and hundreds of rivets will be installed to complete the job, as seen in the photograph at left. (Sacra Studio photograph, Michelle Craig collection.)

While the boiler was being assembled in the boiler shop, the frame and cylinders were being mated together in the main erecting hall. The completed boiler was then moved to the erecting hall and lowered onto the cylinder/frame assembly. The locomotives visible in the above photograph from left to right are numbers 2606, 2607, and 2608. (Sacra Studios photograph, Michelle Craig collection.)

This photograph was taken on the same day as the photograph above. From bottom to top, numbers 2609 and 2608 are little more than bare frames, while numbers 2607 and 2606 both have received their boilers. In the background are several smaller locomotives in the shop for overhauls. (Sam Harrison collection.)

The back wall of the boiler is known as the backhead, and this is where the valves, levers, and gauges required to operate a steam locomotive are installed. Pictured here is the backhead of No. 2600. At least 33 valves are visible, but only seven are labeled. The fireman sits to the left, and the engineer is on the right side of the cab. (IC.)

Most steam locomotives burned coal, which produced cinders. Most cinders fell out of the firebox and onto the ash pan below. However, hot cinders were frequently sucked into the flue pipes running from the firebox to the smokestack. To help break up cinders before they went out the stack, special metal netting was installed in the smoke box. (IC.)

The drivers for a 2600-class locomotive were 70 inches in diameter. A set of drivers have been carefully spotted, and soon the rest of the locomotive will be lowered onto them. Next the rods connecting the drivers will be installed. (Sacra Studio photograph, Michelle Craig collection.)

Newly completed No. 2615 poses next to the Paducah roundhouse on June 25, 1943. After each locomotive was completed, it was sent next door to the roundhouse and fired up. The locomotive was inspected, sent on a test run to Princeton, and inspected again upon return. If everything proved satisfactory, the locomotive was released for service. (Sam Harrison collection.)

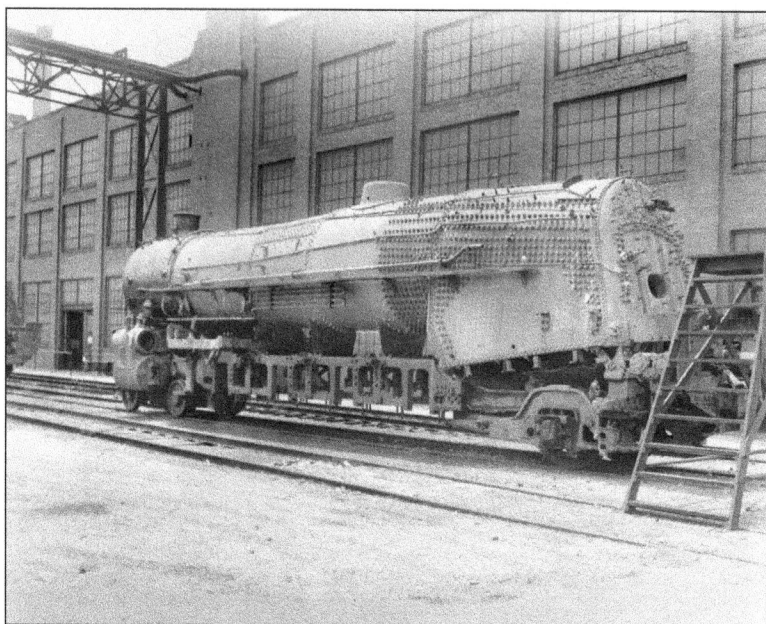

When photographed outside the boiler shop around 1950, 4-8-2 No. 2432 was stripped down to a bare boiler. It was common to see locomotives in such a naked condition being moved between buildings. (Author's collection.)

An often-overlooked department at the Paducah shops was the laboratory. A wide variety of tests were performed here, including checking for minerals or sediments in boiler water that may cause a locomotive to not steam properly. (Sam Harrison collection.)

In an effort to reduce the cost of operating passenger service, in 1925, the IC bought four Brill motorcars. Numbered 117 to 120, these cars had a 175-horsepower gasoline engine mated to a mechanical transmission. The cars proved unreliable and were retired in the 1930s. One car survived until the early 1960s for use as a classroom at the Paducah shops. (Sam Harrison collection.)

It was common for multiple generations to work on the railroad. Seen here around 1955, Hanley Spees (background) works the controls of a portable crane, while E. Goodwin hooks a chain to a locomotive cylinder. Spees's two sons, a brother, and a nephew also worked at the Paducah shops. (Chris Thompson collection.)

During the late 1950s, rail fans flocked to Kentucky to photograph the remaining IC steamers. Among those making the trek was the late Bruce R. Meyer, who ironically later had a long career with the Electro-Motive Division of General Motors (EMD), a major builder of diesel locomotives. Two 2-10-2s and two 4-8-2s await their next call at Paducah on July 15, 1957. (Photograph by Bruce R. Meyer.)

Meyer was an avid model railroader, and during his photographic journeys, he was careful to take close-up photographs of locomotives, cars, and other equipment. This photograph of the front end of 2-10-2 No. 2807 at Paducah is an example of Meyer's meticulous camera work. The top-mounted bell and the headlight in the center of the smokebox door were trademarks of IC steamers. (Photograph by Bruce R. Meyer.)

The 2800-series 2-10-2s were built at Paducah between 1943 and 1945 by mating new boilers to the frames of older 2901-series 2-10-2s. The 2800s exerted nearly 104,000 pounds of tractive effort and were the most powerful steam locomotives ever owned by the IC. (Photograph by Bruce R. Meyer.)

When the 2800s were rebuilt, their tenders were enlarged to carry 19 tons of coal and 12,000 gallons of water. However, these were not the largest tenders on the IC. The tenders behind a 2600-class 4-8-2 carried 26 tons of coal and 22,000 gallons of water. (Photograph by Bruce R. Meyer.)

Following each run, steam locomotives required considerable maintenance. Locomotives were moved around the service area by hostlers. With his hand on the throttle and a careful eye looking forward, this hostler moves 2-10-2 No. 2807 at Paducah on July 15, 1957. Many hostlers were black, but due to racial prejudices, these men had almost no chance of being promoted to engineer. (Photograph by Bruce R. Meyer.)

The coaling tower at the Paducah shops is seen on December 29, 1957. This structure replaced the wooden tower seen on page 37. At the time, there were still many steam locomotives in service on the Kentucky Division, but the GP9 diesel locomotives, visible at right, are evidence that the steam era was going to end in a few short years. (Photograph by Bruce R. Meyer.)

In the foreground, 2-10-2 No. 2731 and 2-8-2 No. 2138 slumber inside the Paducah roundhouse on December 29, 1957. By this date, steam was extinct on many railroads and was quickly disappearing from the IC. The diesels, which replaced steamers, such as numbers 2731 and 2138, required far less maintenance. Thousands of shop workers were laid off across the IC when the railroad finally dieselized. (Photograph by Bruce R. Meyer.)

Bruce Meyer was always on the look out for unusual sights, such as the tender from 4-6-2 No. 1155 sitting forlorn in the Paducah scrap yard on December 29, 1957. No. 1155 had been scrapped the previous summer, and its tender was in storage awaiting conversion as a fuel tender. (Photograph by Bruce R. Meyer.)

Another fan who made the trek to Paducah was Mike Haper, who made his first trip when he was just 14. Since he did not yet have a driver's license, Haper and a rail fan buddy were driven from suburban St. Louis by his mother. One of the first trains they saw after arriving in Paducah was this freight, lead by 2-10-2 No. 2728, pulling into the yard on the evening of October 13, 1956. No. 2728 was built by Lima Locomotive Works in August 1921 and originally was No. 2994. (Photographs by Mike Haper.)

Early the next morning, on October 14, 1956, Haper was at CR Junction just outside of Paducah, where IC's branch line to Barlow split away from the Paducah and Illinois Railroad (P&I). One of the first trains of the day was this freight, lead by 4-8-2 No. 2544, storming into the morning sun toward Paducah. (Photograph by Mike Haper.)

A parade of trains soon materialized, including this long freight powered by 2-10-2 No. 2743, also headed toward Paducah. The bridge in the background carries U.S. Route 60 over the tracks and is located approximately 2 miles east of the present-day Kentucky Oaks Mall. Trains still roll through the junction each day, but the steam locomotives are long gone. (Photograph by Mike Haper.)

57

Not long after No. 2743's train cleared the junction, a westbound coal train pulled by 2-10-2 No. 2721 charged past. The caboose from No. 2743's train is barely visible off to the right. The 2700-class 2-10-2s were common power-on-coal trains and heavy freights throughout much of the system. (Photograph by Mike Haper.)

The 2-10-2 No. 2807 was photographed near the Paducah roundhouse on the morning of October 14, 1956. Mike Haper encountered No. 2807 again on trips to Paducah in November and December 1959. The big 2-10-2 quickly became Haper's favorite steam locomotive, and he later bought the whistle off No. 2807 before the locomotive was scrapped. (Photograph by Mike Haper.)

58

On May 14, 1960, the IC operated a "farewell to steam" excursion from Louisville to Paducah, powered by 4-8-2 No. 2613. Haper traveled to Kentucky to photograph the train and tour the Paducah roundhouse. Other than No. 2613, the only locomotive under steam was 2-10-2 No. 2739, being used as a back-up if No. 2613 failed (it did not). Several other steam locomotives were stored in the roundhouse, ready to go back into service if there was a surge in traffic. One of these locomotives was 4-8-2 No. 2524 (at right). Also inside the roundhouse was Haper's favorite locomotive, 2-10-2 No. 2807 (below). Alas, none of these locomotives ever returned to service. On October 2, 1960, No. 2613 powered another excursion between Louisville and Dawson Springs, ending 109 years of steam locomotive service on the IC. (Photographs by Mike Haper.)

All but a handful of IC steamers were scrapped, including trim 2-6-0 No. 475, pictured at Paducah in May 1955. Built in 1895, this locomotive had a Belpaire firebox, a rarity on the IC. (Photograph by C. Ulrich, author's collection.)

In the mid-1950s, the storage tracks next to the Paducah shops were filled with dead steamers awaiting the torch. Most IC steamers were scrapped by the railroad at Paducah. The railroad earned more money by doing the scrapping themselves rather than selling locomotives intact to scrap dealers. Scrapping a locomotive generally took between 270 and 280 man-hours. (Author's collection.)

Most, if not all, of the famed 2600-class 4-8-2s were scrapped at Paducah. No. 2606 awaits a date with the scrapper's torch in early 1960. To the right is the same training car seen on page 51. The tenders from many retired steam locomotives were saved and rebuilt to haul fuel oil and sand. (Sam Harrison collection.)

To the casual observer, the scrap yard at Paducah was a chaotic, unorganized mess. But in reality, it was a well-organized and efficient operation. There were several storage tracks, plus two tracks where locomotives were actually scrapped. Crews moved along the scrap tracks, cutting up locomotives in a methodical order. Once all locomotives on the scrap track were dismantled, the track was restocked. (Sam Harrison collection.)

The first step in scrapping a steamer was removing the cab, followed by the sheet metal jacket and asbestos surrounding the boiler. Next, as seen in this photograph at left, the top half of the boiler was cut away, revealing the flues. These long pipes were cut loose and removed, tied in large bundles, and set aside for the trip to the steel mill. (Sam Harrison collection.)

Most locomotives were scrapped without using a single wrench, hammer, or hand tool. Instead, workers relied almost exclusively on acetylene torches. Below, two workers are seen cutting apart the top half of the boiler from 2-8-2 No. 1504. (Sam Harrison collection.)

Working in a precise, orderly fashion, the scrappers quickly carved apart the carcass of each condemned steamer. The pieces were laid to the side, where they were sorted and loaded into gondolas. The frame and drivers are all that is left of this unidentified 2-8-2, but soon even these parts will be gone. (Sam Harrison collection.)

Each driver had several hundred pounds of lead used as counterbalance. To reclaim this metal, the drivers were set on this rack and the axles were cut off. Next the drivers were put into a furnace. The lead melted away and was poured into ingots. (Sam Harrison collection.)

Looking somewhat like an outlandish flower planter, the sand dome from 2-8-2 No. 1360 rests in front of the Paducah storehouse. Scrap prices dictated the speed at which the scrappers worked. When scrap prices were high, extra crews were often put to work. But by early 1962, the remaining steamers were gone, leaving only photographs and memories in their wake. (Sam Harrison collection.)

One of the few IC steamers to escape the scraper's torch was 2-8-2 No. 1518. It was put on display in 1964 in Barkley Park on the banks of the Ohio River. On May 7, 1985, the locomotive moved to the foot of Broadway next to the floodwall. Exactly 14 years later, it moved two blocks to its present location between Kentucky and Washington Streets. (Chris Thompson collection.)

In addition to the shops, the IC had many other interesting facilities in Paducah. One of them was the icehouse, seen here on November 20, 1921. This wooden structure was located near Union Station. For several decades, strawberries were shipped from IC's downtown freight house, and the icehouse was used to cool down the cars before loading. (IC.)

The wooden structure at the top of the page gave way to a new brick structure. The 4-8-2 No. 2520 leads a westbound-loaded coal train past the icehouse on December 28, 1957. By that date, the building was used only sporadically to replenish the ice supply in railroad reefers, and most production was going to retail customers. (Photograph by Bruce R. Meyer.)

Another notable structure in Paducah was Union Station, located off Brown Street in the Littleville section of the city. Opened in early 1900, the structure originally measured 196-by-28 feet. In late 1917, construction began on a 56-by-28-foot addition to the north end of the building to house a lunchroom and expanded baggage room. This photograph was taken on October 24, 1917. (Sam Harrison collection.)

Canopies over the platforms on both sides of the building were also added, as seen on December 18, 1917. Although built and owned by the IC, the depot was also used by the Nashville, Chattanooga, and St. Louis Railway (NC&StL), which reached Paducah via a branch line from Bruceton, Tennessee. The IC used the tracks in the foreground, while NC&StL used the tracks on the other side of the building. (IC.)

The interior of the new lunchroom is seen on March 6, 1918. Customers were greeted by white tablecloths, cakes, bananas, and assorted goodies. In addition to train passengers, the lunchroom was patronized by workers of nearby businesses. (IC.)

NC&StL's 4-6-0 No. 250 poses next to Paducah Union Station about 1940. The NC&StL discontinued passenger service to Paducah on March 31, 1951. Then, on January 29, 1957, the IC ran its last passenger trains through Paducah. Afterwards, the building was used as office space until it was demolished in 1964. (Author's collection.)

Many major railroads operated their own hospitals to care for injured and sick employees. The IC had three hospitals, located in Paducah, Chicago, and New Orleans. The Paducah hospital was established on January 15, 1884, by the CO&SW and was inherited by the IC with the 1896 takeover of the CO&SW. It was the first modern hospital established in Paducah and the first hospital in the IC system. The hospital was originally housed in the elegant two-story brick and wooden structure seen here. The front of the building (above) faced Broadway, while the rear of the structure (below) bordered Jefferson Street. With its tall, white columns and large lawn, the hospital was a well-known landmark in Paducah. Both photographs on this page were taken on June 21, 1915. (Both, IC.)

Behind the hospital was a stable used to house the horses that pulled the hospital's ambulance. In an effort to provide faster service, in 1908, a second ambulance (also horse drawn) was purchased and housed at a private stable downtown at Fourth Street and Kentucky Avenue. (Sam Harrison collection.)

In 1914, a motorized ambulance was purchased, providing patients with a much faster ride to the hospital than via the slow horse-drawn ambulance. As with most cars and trucks of the era, the new ambulance left the driver almost totally exposed to the elements. (IC.)

On July 10, 1917, the IC hospital caught fire and burned to the ground. Replacing the hospital was a slow process, and construction of the new building did not begin until mid-1918. The above photograph was taken in the fall of 1918, while the photograph below was taken on January 28, 1919. Wartime shortages of men and materials slowed construction, and the hospital did not open until December 6, 1919. After losing money for several years, the hospital closed in 1957 and was sold to local businessman George Katterjohn. The building housed medical offices and was known as the Katterjohn building even after Katterjohn sold it. Citing the need for expensive repairs, the owners closed the building in October 2007. In 2010, it sits empty, facing an uncertain future. (Above, IC; below, Sam Harrison collection.)

The IC had a large and diverse list of customers around Paducah. One major shipper was the General Tire and Rubber plant in Mayfield, about 20 miles south of Paducah. Only a small portion of the plant is visible in this publicity photograph, taken about 1965. Over the years, the plant was expanded several times until it ultimately covered 2.25 million square feet. The plant was the largest employer in Graves County, and at times, employment topped 2,000. General Tire was acquired by the German tire conglomerate Continental in 1987. In September 1998, the author went to work at the plant and remained there until December 2004, when tire production was suspended. Until 2007, a small portion of the plant remained open to mix rubber for other Continental General plants. (Hedrich-Blessing photograph.)

Beginning in the 1950s, a large complex of chemical plants was built near the small town of Calvert City, about 20 miles east of Paducah. The plants provided thousands of jobs to area residents and an immense amount of freight to the IC. GP18 No. 9404 is surrounded by tank cars as it switches at one of the plants around 1963. (Author's collection.)

Around 1964, a switch crew poses for a publicity photograph in front of the B. F. Goodrich plant. Most of the plants are located along the Tennessee River north of the IC mainline. A tangled web of sidings and storage yards was laid throughout Calvert City to service the plants. (Hedrich-Blessing photograph.)

72

In 1966, the famed Civil War locomotive the *General* visited the annual meeting of the Southern Governor's Conference, held on September 18–20 at Kentucky Dam Village State Park. This diminutive locomotive became an instant celebrity on April 12, 1862, after Union raiders stole it during a breakfast stop at Big Shanty, Georgia, (later renamed Kennesaw). The raiders then headed north toward Tennessee. Their goal was to destroy track along the way and sever a key supply route to the Confederacy. The plan failed, and eight of the raiders were executed. After years of display at Chattanooga (Tennessee) Union Station, the *General* was restored to operating condition in 1962 by its owner, the Louisville and Nashville Railroad (L&N). The locomotive subsequently toured much of the southeast under its own power. (Both, Chris Thompson collection.)

Delegates to the governors' conference, numerous school kids, and a few lucky members of the general public were treated to short rides behind the *General*. The photographs on pages 73 and 74 were all taken at IC's Grand Rivers depot, which served as the operations base for the excursions. Train crews dressed in Civil War clothing, as seen on the left. Also attending the conference was Miss America Vicki Hurd, photographed below while sitting at the throttle. These 1966 trips turned out to be the last time that the *General* was ever under steam. Afterwards, the L&N became entangled in a lengthy court battle with the City of Chattanooga, Tennessee, over ownership of the locomotive. The L&N prevailed and subsequently donated the locomotive in 1967 to a museum in Kennesaw, Georgia, where it remains on display today. (Both, Chris Thompson collection.)

Four

HOPKINSVILLE-PRINCETON-HENDERSON

During the late 1800s, hundreds of new railroads were proposed in Kentucky. Most of these projects died either due to lack of funding or poor management. One project that did get off the ground was the Ohio Valley Railroad and Mining Company. This project was conceived by Dr. P. G. Kelsey, who operated a coal mine near DeKoven. Kelsey had visions of building a railroad from Henderson south to Jackson, Tennessee.

Kelsey began construction of his new road at Henderson in 1886, and by late 1887, the line had reached Princeton, 88 miles to the south. In 1888, the road was renamed the Ohio Valley Railroad (OV). In 1891, the OV was purchased by the CO&SW but continued operations under its own name. The tracks were extended south to Hopkinsville in 1892, at which point all construction ceased. In 1896, both the CO&SW and OV were bought by the IC. The tracks were then made part of the Evansville District.

The Evansville District expanded in 1968 when the IC bought the Hopkinsville-Nashville segment of the bankrupt Tennessee Central Railway. But by that time, the line was facing hard times, and beginning in 1981, parts of the line were either sold or abandoned. In early 1986, the line from Gracey south to Hopkinsville was sold to the C&J Railroad, but the new railroad lasted less than two years before failing. Today the only remaining segments of the Evansville District are 9 miles of track north of Princeton operated by the Fredonia Valley Railroad. The U.S. Army also operates approximately 17 miles of track south from Hopkinsville to serve the sprawling Fort Campbell army base.

The IC's passenger depot at Hopkinsville was located along Ninth Street on the banks of the Little River. Three dapper gentlemen pose in front of the depot around 1905. As required by state law, the depot has separate waiting rooms for white and black passengers. (Author's collection.)

Much of the trackage between Hopkinsville and Hendersonville was built by the OV, including this bridge across the Little River near Hopkinsville, photographed on February 12, 1898. The structure measured an even 100 feet from end to end. Like many bridges on the former OV, it was replaced after the IC took over the line. (IC.)

The Hopkinsville-Henderson mainline intersected the IC's Paducah-Louisville line at Princeton. For several decades, the Princeton depot was a beehive of activity. Two passenger trains are visible in this February 12, 1898, photograph. At the end of the depot is a dining room to feed hungry passengers. (Author's collection.)

The wooden depot seen at the top of this page was ultimately replaced by this two-story brick structure, photographed on October 17, 1957. The bottom floor was used by passengers, while the top floor was used as office space. Passenger service between Fulton and Louisville ended on January 29, 1957, and afterwards, most depots on this route were demolished, including the one at Princeton. (Author's collection.)

In early 1914, the IC began construction of a new roundhouse at Princeton, replacing an older structure dating back to the 1800s. The above photograph was taken on June 26, 1914, as the back wall of the roundhouse was taking shape. Construction was complete, and the locomotive was seeing daily use when the photograph below was taken on October 30, 1914. There were six stalls, and it was used to maintain locomotives on both the Evansville and Paducah Districts. After the IC quit using steam locomotives in 1960, the roundhouse remained open but with a greatly reduced workforce. Finally, around 1964, the roundhouse was replaced by a new diesel shop and afterwards was torn down. (Both, Sam Harrison collection.)

The storehouse at the Princeton roundhouse is pictured on April 28, 1915. When the Princeton roundhouse was demolished, both the storehouse and the adjacent powerhouse were spared. The structures subsequently were used by a grain elevator but are now being used as a recycling center. (Sam Harrison collection.)

A wooden tipple at Sturgis owned by an unidentified mine was photographed on May 7, 1918. A chute on the right side of the tipple loaded coal into hoppers parked on the siding. Meanwhile, a second chute was used to load coal directly into the tenders of steam locomotives parked on the mainline. (Sam Harrison collection.)

MORGANFIELD, K.Y.
Passenger Station

Morganfield is located 35.1 rail miles north of Princeton. Here the IC's Evansville District meets the Uniontown District, a 6-mile-long branch line running north to Uniontown. Depots in smaller towns and cities along the IC were usually built from wood, but the Morganfield depot was of stucco construction. The bulletin on the wall lists three trains daily on the Evansville District and four daily on the Uniontown District. Passenger service ended on the Uniontown District on January 1, 1929, and on the Evansville District on February 13, 1941. Both photographs were taken on December 17, 1923. (Both, author's collection.)

MORGANFIELD, K.Y.
Passenger Station

Around 1950, an IC train powered by 2-8-2 No. 1816 heads south past the L&N depot at Henderson. IC trains used the L&N's bridge to cross the Ohio River at Henderson. (Author's collection.)

ILL. CENT. TOWER
HENDERSON, KY.

The junction between the IC and the L&N in Henderson was controlled by this wooden interlocking tower. It was built and maintained by the IC and staffed by IC employees. When the tower was photographed about 1960, the IC logo on the front of the structure was badly faded and barely visible. Eventually the junction was replaced by automated equipment, and the tower was razed. (Author's collection.)

Seen here around 1905, a switch crew at Henderson poses next to 0-6-0 No. 2574, built in 1889 by Baldwin for the OV. After the IC took over the OV in 1897, the locomotive was renumbered several times before being sold in 1916. (John B. Allen collection.)

Although the IC had only minimal maintenance facilities at Henderson, the railroad did have a small shop facility just across the Ohio River at Evansville, Indiana. A portion of the shops are seen here on January 30, 1917. (Sam Harrison collection.)

Five

KING COAL

During the 1900s, the coal industry was often referred to as "King Coal." That title was certainly appropriate, for tens of thousands of Kentuckians worked in coal mines spread across the western and eastern regions of the state. The coal industry had a major impact on Kentucky's economy and politics. When the owner or president of a major coal mine spoke, politicians, from mayors all the way to the governor, listened.

The IC benefited greatly from the coal industry. In 1937, the IC served 38 coal mines in western Kentucky. The IC hauled 3,000,000 tons of "black diamonds" from these mines. This business generated approximately $4.8 million for the railroad. Coal from western Kentucky was shipped by rail throughout the Midwest and Deep South. Customers included steel mills, factories, electric generating plants, and homeowners. Another major customer was the railroad industry itself. During the 1920s, steam locomotives burned approximately one-third of all coal mined in the United States.

During the 1960s, production in the western Kentucky coal fields began to fall sharply. Coal from the area is high in sulfur, and many customers were forced to switch to cleaner-burning coal from Wyoming to comply with strict new environmental laws. Most mines have since closed, including Peabody's River Queen Mine east of Central City, once one of the biggest mines in the region. A handful of mines still operate, but the King Coal era is dead.

The first coal mines in western Kentucky were small, underground operations. In the mid-1900s, several companies adopted the highly controversial strip-mining method. Massive shovels first stripped away the dirt covering the coal deposits, and smaller shovels then removed the coal. The largest strip-mining shovel in western Kentucky was employed at Peabody's Sinclair Mine near Drakesboro. Built by the Bucyrus-Erie Company, the parts were shipped to the mine aboard 300 rail cars. The massive shovel took 11 months to assemble, weighed 18 million pounds, was 220 feet tall, and could pick up 115 cubic yards of dirt at a time. Nicknamed the "Big Hog," the shovel entered service in 1962 and was retired in the mid-1980s. "Big Hog" was too big to move to another mine and too expensive to scrap; instead, it was buried on-site. (Hedrich-Blessing photograph.)

Another large strip mine operated by Peabody Coal was the River Queen Mine, located east of Central City. Seen in 1959, a shovel built by the Marion Power Shovel Company loads coal onto a Euclid coal hauler. Meanwhile, in the background, a Bucyrus Model 1650-B shovel strips away the earth. (IC.)

Two haulers are seen unloading their black diamonds into a long trough at the River Queen Mine. The Euclid coal haulers were equipped with bottom dump hoppers that unloaded faster than traditional trucks. Two of these haulers could fill a standard railroad hopper, which at the time hauled between 50 and 70 tons. (IC.)

The coal was then sent to the tipple, where it was washed, sorted by size, and cleaned of debris, such as rocks and dirt. Next the coal was dumped into railroad hoppers. Most coal mined at River Queen was hauled away by the IC. But Peabody Coal also operated its own private railroad to a dock on the Green River, where coal was loaded onto barges. (IC.)

The vantage point of this 1959 photograph is the roof of a 9300-series GP9 parked in IC's Madisonville yard. Traditionally, Madisonville was the busiest station on the Kentucky Division. During the 1950s, it was not uncommon for 500 carloads of coal to originate at Madisonville each day. Moving the loaded cars was important but so was moving empty cars back to the mine for reloading. (IC.)

Prior to the 1970s, most railroad freight cars were equipped with plain bearings on their axles. These required frequent lubrication, and even with diligent maintenance, they were prone to overheating. At Madisonville, a car inspector is pictured around 1960 initialing a car that he just lubricated. (IC.)

Once the cars have been loaded and inspected, they are assembled into trains and hauled to the customer. On January 29, 1959, a loaded coal train heads east on the new line through Madisonville. The signals in the background are at milepost JK 146.5, approximately 1 mile east of Madisonville's West Yard. (IC.)

In an effort to improve safety and boost productivity, 14 steam locomotives assigned to coal field service at Madisonville were equipped with radios during 1954. A cigar-chomping engineer demonstrates the operation of the new equipment, which was installed in the cab behind the engineer's seat. (IC.)

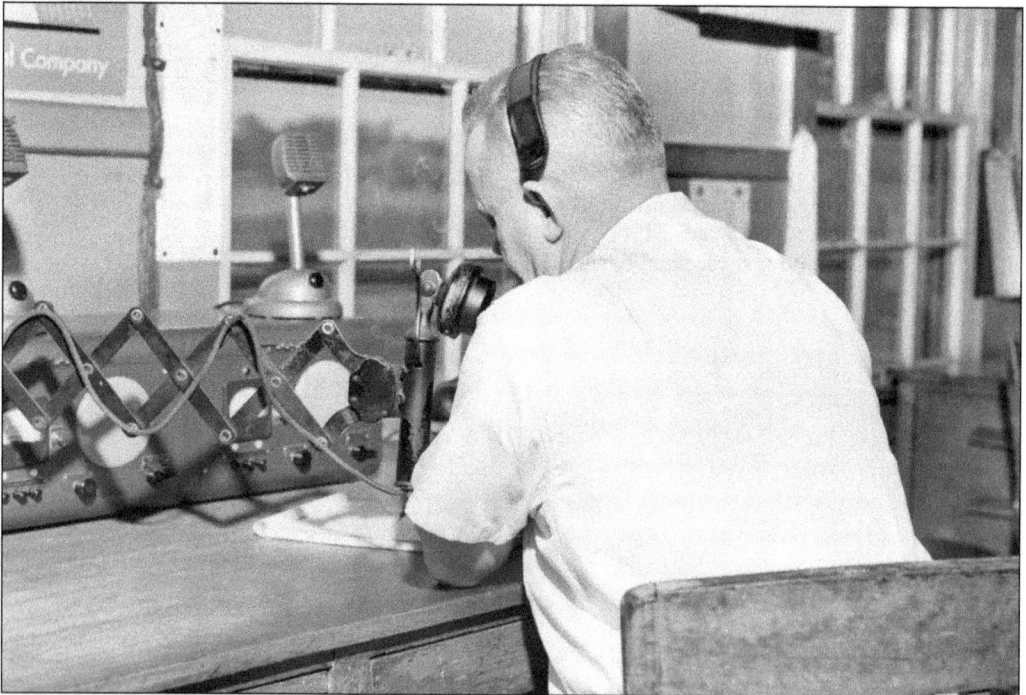

Radios were also installed in the depots at Madisonville and Central City. Assistant trainmaster Carl Rogers is pictured on August 17, 1954, while talking on the company telephone at the IC's Madisonville depot. The telephone's scissor handset partially obscures the radio set at the rear of Rogers's desk. (IC.)

The IC competed
fiercely against the
L&N for business in
the western Kentucky
coalfields. Tracks of the
two railroads intersected
at several locations,
including at Nortonville,
approximately 72 rail
miles east of Paducah.
Initially the IC and L&N
had separate depots
at Nortonville. These
were consolidated into
the depot seen here,
photographed about 1905.
(Author's collection.)

Many railroads owned their own coal companies. The goal was to ensure an uninterrupted supply
of coal for the railroad's locomotives. In 1900, the IC bought the Madison Coal Corporation and
its vast coal holdings in western Kentucky and southern Illinois. Afterwards, IC bought most of
its coal from Madison Coal. The 2-8-2 No. 1807 pauses at Central City in 1924 to take on coal.
(Author's collection.)

During the 1960s, the coal business was dramatically transformed with the introduction of unit coal trains. These trains typically ran 75 to 100 cars in length. All cars were loaded at a single mine and destined to a single customer, usually a utility plant. In the above photograph, a unit coal train stands to the left while a locomotive stares down the photographer. The photograph below was taken at the same location but from a different vantage point. Both photographs were taken in mid-1968 near the Kentucky Dam. Pulling the train is a pair of brand new U33C locomotives built in April 1968. (Hedrich-Blessing photographs.)

Six

CENTRAL CITY–LOUISVILLE

The Louisville District of the Kentucky Division ran from Central City to Louisville, a distance of 126 miles. Coal accounted for much of the traffic on the Louisville District, but a significant amount of tobacco also traveled over the district. During the 1930s, Louisville was home to two of the largest cigarette plants in the country. Together these plants produced approximately 12 billion cigarettes annually.

Bourbon whiskey was another notable product hauled by the IC. After Prohibition ended in 1933, dozens of distilleries sprang up across central Kentucky. By the mid-1930s, there were 12 distilleries operating in the Louisville area, with eight being served by the IC.

Approximately 30 miles south of Louisville is Fort Knox. Although best known for its fortresslike gold vault, since the early 1930s, Fort Knox has also served as a major training center for army tank crews. Until the late 1950s, trains carried troops to and from the base. The base still has a rail link to the outside world, which is used for receiving and shipping heavy equipment.

Louisville, the state's largest city, was served during the mid-1900s by eight Class 1 railroads, including the IC. Downtown, the IC owned Central Station, a massive passenger terminal used by the Southern Railway, the New York Central Railroad, the Chesapeake and Ohio Railway, and the Baltimore and Ohio Railroad. In 1957, IC ended passenger service to Louisville, but Central Station survived until 1969, when it was demolished to make way for an interstate highway.

The freight yard and engine house at Central City are seen in this rare photograph, taken in July 1918. This view is looking east toward Louisville. Cars and locomotives were repaired in

the wooden buildings in the photograph to the left of the page. Note that there is no turntable. Instead, locomotives were turned by running them around the wye track behind the engine house. (Author's collection.)

ENGINE HOUSE LOOKING EAST
MECHANICAL TERMINAL
CENTRAL CITY KY.
JULY 1918.

Derailments and collisions were quite common in the railroad industry during the early 1900s. Railroads kept specially equipped trains at major terminals, ready at a moment's notice to clear up the mess and get trains rolling again. The Central City wreck train is visible in the center of this photograph next to the two-track engine house. (Author's collection.)

ENGINE HOUSE & MACHINE SHOP LOOKING N.W.
MECHANICAL TERMINAL
CENTRAL CITY KENTUCKY
JULY 1918.

The shops at Central City are seen one more time on July 1918, this time looking to the west. Four kids can be seen walking toward the camera on the right side of the photograph. Trains have always been a fascination for kids, but playing around railroad equipment can result in injury or death. (Author's collection.)

In 1924, the IC completed a new 42-mile-long line running from Central City westward through Madisonville to Dawson Springs. As part of this project, a new freight yard and locomotive service facilities were constructed at Central City. Construction of the new 12-stall roundhouse was drawing to a conclusion in the photograph above. Meanwhile, considerable work still needed to be done on the new coaling tower, seen in the photograph below. The coaling tower was built of concrete, and the wooden framework was used to support the concrete forms. Both photographs were taken on April 22, 1924. (Both, IC.)

On September 28, 1928, an anonymous photographer captured this scene of 2-8-0 No. 919 taking coal at Central City. To the casual observer, the Central City coaling tower was a lifeless structure whose only purpose was to refuel the coal bunkers of hungry steam locomotives. But the tower helped spark the author's lifelong interest in trains. During the mid-1980s, the author and his father visited Central City countless times to photograph trains next to the coaling tower. Steam had been gone for more than two decades, the ground was soaked with diesel fuel and lubricating oil, and many locomotives were grungy and dirty. Yet there were always many interesting locomotives to be found. Each visit reinforced the author's interest in railroads and the IC in particular. (John B. Allen collection.)

The 2-10-2 No. 2740 eases up to the coaling tower late on the afternoon of May 18, 1956. No. 2740 was one of forty-nine 2700-series 2-10-2s turned out by the Paducah shops between 1943 and 1945. These locomotives were rebuilt from older 2901-series 2-10-2s, with higher boiler pressure and larger tenders. (Conniff Railroadiana collection.)

Drastic changes were on the horizon when this June 29, 1986, photograph was taken near the Central City coaling tower. On August 27, 1986, the Paducah and Louisville Railway bought most of the IC's Kentucky Division, and within months, the locomotive facility at Central City was shut down. The tracks and buildings are gone, but the coaling tower still remains, along with the memories. (Author's photograph.)

In 1954, the route between Chicago and Omaha, Nebraska, was dieselized with new GP9s. Some of the displaced steamers were reassigned to the Kentucky Division, including several of the 2800-class 2-10-2s. No. 2816 looms large at Central City on July 16, 1957. (Photograph by Bruce R. Meyer.)

Other transplants included the 2600-class 4-8-2s. These locomotives were originally assigned to service between Chicago and North Cairo, but when that line was dieselized in 1956, several of these locomotives moved south to the Kentucky Division. On a blustery winter day around 1957, a westbound freight behind No. 2614 rolls out of the yard at Central City. (Author's collection.)

Between 1911 and 1923, the IC accumulated a fleet of more than five hundred 2-8-2 Mikado locomotives. These locomotives were outnumbered only by the ubiquitous 4-4-0s of the mid-1800s. The 2-8-2 No. 1599 awaits its next run inside the Central City roundhouse on July 16, 1957. (Photograph by Bruce R. Meyer.)

In early 1959, the IC withdrew all remaining steamers from service. Many locomotives were "stored serviceable," including 2-8-2 No. 1572, photographed at Central City on August 28, 1959, with its stack covered. Later, in 1959, several steamers were recalled for service out of Paducah but not No. 1572. It never ran again and was scrapped around 1961. The roundhouse also did not survive; it was torn down in 1960. (Author's collection.)

Caneyville was served by this steel tower, photographed around 1920 shortly after its construction. The tower had two chutes, including one to refuel locomotives parked on the mainline, which is the track on the right side. Another chute could refuel locomotives on the siding passing underneath the storage bin. (Sam Harrison collection.)

Cecilia was the junction between the Central City–Louisville mainline and the Hodgenville District, a 17-mile-long branch line that ran through Elizabethtown before terminating at Hodgenville. Railroad facilities included a depot, stock pens, and this wooden coaling tower that serviced locomotives on both the mainline and the branch. Photographed on July 3, 1916, the tower was later replaced by a larger structure. (Sam Harrison collection.)

In 1936, the U.S. Treasury Department opened the U.S. Bullion Depository at Fort Knox, better known simply as the "gold vault." Between 1937 and 1941, a total of 84 heavily fortified trains moved stockpiles of gold bars to Fort Knox from the Philadelphia Mint and the Federal Reserve Bank in New York City. These trains took several different routes to Louisville, but the only rail link between Louisville and Fort Knox is via the IC. In the above photograph, a "gold train" sits in the siding at Fort Knox while trucks loaded with the precious metal head for the vault. The photograph below was taken at the front gate to the vault. The gold was shipped as registered mail aboard specially equipped baggage cars. (Both, author's collection.)

In addition to transporting gold, the IC moved thousands of soldiers to and from Fort Knox. Some of these soldiers traveled aboard regularly scheduled passenger trains, but the IC also operated numerous troop trains. Around 1958, a troop train rolls up to the platform at Fort Knox, with a 2400-series 4-8-2 on the point. (Author's collection.)

Troop trains were typically pulled by 4-6-2s or 2400-class 4-8-2s, which were designed and built for passenger service. However, any type of locomotive was used when they were in short supply. On June 29, 1956, a troop train was photographed at Fort Knox with 2-10-2 No. 2713. The 2-10-2s were more at home hauling coal drags and heavy freights. (Author's collection.)

Louisville Depot Fire May 1909.

In 1884, the CO&SW opened a small passenger terminal in Louisville on the banks of the Ohio River. The road later began construction of a much larger one, but it was destroyed by a tornado on March 27, 1890. The building finally opened in 1891 but was heavily damaged in early 1909 by fire, as seen here in May 1909. (Sam Harrison collection.)

Depot & Water St. Louisville, Ky.

During reconstruction after the 1909 fire, the small hillside on the west side of the terminal was removed, the tower was rebuilt, and much of the structure on the south side was remodeled. Reconstruction was well underway when this undated photograph was taken. (Sam Harrison collection.)

LOUISVILLE KY. PASS. STATION.

The rebuilt station is seen here about 1915. On the side of the tower is a sign reading, "Union Depot," the structure's original name. This created confusion with Union Station, the L&N's passenger terminal at Tenth Street and Broadway, so the IC building was eventually renamed Central Station. (Chris Thompson collection.)

RESCUEING AN OFFICER AT UNION DEPOT FLOOD APRIL 1913 LOUISVILLE KY. (R.R.)

During most years, floodwaters on the adjacent Ohio River were a nuisance rather than a major problem. But during the spring of 1913, the river swamped the station with nearly 5 feet of water. This real-photo postcard is captioned, "Rescuing an officer at Union Depot. Flood April 1913 Louisville, KY." (Author's collection.)

An even greater flood hit the station in January and February 1937. At the height of the flood, the entire first floor was submerged all the way to the ceiling. Once the waters receded, several weeks were needed to repair the station. Many of the tracks behind the structure were twisted like pretzels. (Sam Harrison collection.)

In an effort to reduce maintenance costs, the third and fourth floors of Louisville's Central Station were removed in 1944, along with the tower. The truncated station was photographed on February 16, 1945. IC passenger service to Louisville ended on January 29, 1957, and Central Station was demolished in 1969. (IC.)

Turntable.

IC's main freight yard in Louisville was located at Oak Street, about 2 miles west of downtown. Adjacent to the yard was a roundhouse, where 4-6-2 No. 1048 was photographed on March 11, 1916. The 4-6-2 was common power for IC's passenger trains from the early 1900s until larger 4-8-2 locomotives arrived in the 1920s. (IC.)

Machine Shop & Power House.

The machine shop and powerhouse are next to the Louisville roundhouse, as seen on March 11, 1916, with 2-8-0 No. 606 in the foreground. In early 1958, the IC dieselized the Louisville District. Afterwards, the Louisville roundhouse was demolished, but the turntable was kept to turn locomotives. (IC.)

Seven

HORSE BRANCH–
OWENSBORO

The Owensboro District dates back to 1882 when the Owensboro, Falls of Rough, and Green River Railroad (OFR&GR) was chartered to lay track from Owensboro through the small community of Falls of Rough and onward to an unspecified point on the Green River. On October 1, 1887, the line from Owensboro south to Fordsville opened for business.

In 1892, Collis P. Huntington took over the OFR&GR and, in 1893, extended the line to Horse Branch, where it connected with the CO&SW, also owned by Huntington. Alas the OFR&GR entered receivership in 1894 and, in 1897, was merged into the IC.

At Owensboro, the IC had a freight house and small yard. The IC even shared Union Station, built in 1905 on Frederica Street, with the L&N. Several factories in Owensboro were served by the IC, but otherwise, the rest of the line passed through rural countryside and the occasional small town. Passenger service on the line ended on July 23, 1928.

For years, a freight line ran daily between Horse Branch and Owensboro, but traffic fell steadily during the 1970s, and the line was abandoned in 1981. Some of the trackage in Owensboro was taken over by the L&N, but the rest of the line was torn up.

During the 1940s and 1950s, trains on the Owensboro District were frequently pulled by 4-6-2 No. 2099. This locomotive was built in 1902 as 2-6-2 No. 1001, the only 2-6-2 ever owned by the IC. In 1907, the locomotive was rebuilt as 4-6-2 No. 1000 and, in 1943, was rebuilt again and renumbered as No. 2099. Here, on May 1, 1957, No. 2099 prepares to leave Owensboro with a southbound freight. (John B. Allen collection.)

At Whitesville, No. 2099 and its train cut through the woods. Trackage on the Owensboro District cut through undulating terrain and had numerous curves. For southbound trains, Whitesville was near the summit of a 2-mile climb that began near the small community of Haynes. (John B. Allen collection.)

No. 2099 is photographed one more time at Fordsville. This small town was once served by a branch line of the L&N running from Fordsville north to Irvington. Traffic on this L&N line dried up during the 1930s and was abandoned in 1941, along with another L&N branch line running from Ellmitch (just east of Fordsville) south to Hartford. (John B. Allen collection.)

In January 1958, steam locomotives were replaced on the Owensboro District by diesel locomotives. GP18 No. 9427 is photographed here around 1965, leading a short train past a quarry. (IC.)

During the mid-1900s the IC replaced many of its older depots with new structures built to a standard design. One of the new depots was constructed at Horse Branch, photographed here about 1960. IC's Paducah-Louisville mainline is out of view in the foreground, while the hoppers in the background are sitting on the Owensboro District. (Author's collection.)

The IC maintained a wooden freight house and small freight yard along Second Street in Owensboro, photographed about 1960. The tracks continued a few hundred yards farther before terminating on the banks of the Ohio River. (John B. Allen collection.)

Eight

BRIDGES

Bridges are usually seen as cold, inanimate objects. However, bridges also have the power to change history. As an example, consider the IC's bridge across the Ohio River at Cairo, Illinois. By 1876, the IC had expanded its system all the way south to New Orleans. But cars and locomotives had to be ferried across the Ohio River. The slow ferries limited the amount of passengers and freight the IC could handle.

In mid-1887, construction began on a bridge at Cairo. With great fanfare, the bridge opened on October 29, 1889. The final cost was set at $2,675,457.92, or roughly $200,000 over budget. Few IC officials grumbled about the extra cost, for almost immediately the railroad experienced a traffic boom. In 1890, the IC hauled 6.3 million tons of freight, but by 1900, that figure was up to 18.1 million tons. This boom cannot be attributed entirely to the Cairo bridge, for the IC added hundreds of miles of track during this period. But it was obvious that thanks to the bridge, the IC was picking up a great deal of business.

The Cairo bridge took many beating over the years. In 1911, it was strengthened to allow the safe passage of new 2-8-2 Mikado locomotives. Then, in 1934 and 1935, the steel approach trestle on the south side of the bridge was replaced. The most dramatic change took place between 1950 and 1952, when the spans over the river were replaced.

Other notable IC bridges in Kentucky included drawbridges over the Tennessee, Cumberland, and Green Rivers. Several large, steel trestles were also erected to overcome the rugged terrain on the Louisville District. Perhaps the most famous trestle was on Muldraugh Hill, approximately 23 miles west of Louisville. The cover photograph was taken at this curving steel bridge, which measures 704 feet long and 127 feet high.

Perhaps the most famous bridge on the entire IC spanned the Ohio River at Cairo, Illinois. Construction began in early 1887, and the bridge opened for business on October 29, 1889. The bridge cost $2.6 million, a sizeable sum for the era. The money was well spent, for completion of the bridge helped spark a traffic boom during the 1890s. (IC.)

This view of the Cairo bridge was taken about 1935 from an observation car on the rear of a passenger train. Railroad officials often boasted that the bridge was 4 miles long. That claim was a bit of a stretch, for the nine spans of the main superstructure measured 4,583 feet. On each side of the bridge, there were approximately 7,800 feet of steel and wooden trestles. (Author's collection.)

In 1905 and 1906, most of the trestle on the Illinois side of the Cairo bridge was replaced by a massive earthen embankment. A few years later, the trestle on the south side of the bridge began to rust. Replacement of the entire south trestle and the remaining segment of the north trestle began in mid-1934. Concrete pillars to support the new trestle are seen under construction on September 19, 1934. (IC.)

Steel towers were then erected atop the concrete pillars, followed by large box girders that supported the track. These girders were constructed on the Kentucky side and then moved into position by a railroad derrick. Here, on Halloween in 1934, one of the girders is lowered onto the steel towers below. The new trestle was completed in February 1935, and a few months later the old trestle was dismantled. (IC.)

Once the approach trestles were replaced, the only segments of the original 1889 bridge remaining were the nine spans of the superstructure. Because of the bridge's frail condition, trains faced speed and weight restrictions. In 1949, the IC's board of directors voted to spend $6.3 million to rebuild the bridge. Engineers adopted a construction method that had never been attempted on such a large size. First, each new span was constructed on a barge anchored next to the old bridge. In the above photograph, the bottom deck of a new span has been laid, along with ties and rails. The photograph at left shows the span once the side and top beams were installed. (Both, author's collection.)

Reconstruction of the Cairo bridge began with the span closest to the Illinois shore and then moved across the river toward Kentucky. The bridge remained open throughout the reconstruction project, except for a period of approximately 24 hours when each span was replaced. First, the old span was pulled out of the way until it rested on temporary steel piers. Next the new span was pulled into position. Once the rails were bolted together and signal wires were connected, the bridge reopened to traffic. The old spans were then stripped down to their bare frames and dropped into the Ohio River. Divers cut up the old spans, and the scrap was hauled away to steel mills for recycling. (Hedrich-Blessing photographs.)

In 1923, the IC purchased a one-third share of the Paducah and Illinois Railroad, including its bridge across the Ohio River at Metropolis, Illinois. Construction of the P&I bridge began in August 1914, but due to financial issues, work on the bridge was abruptly halted on September 14, 1914. (However, track laying between Paducah and the bridge site was allowed to continue.) Work on the bridge resumed in July 1915, and the structure officially opened for business on January 1, 1918. Both of these photographs were taken about 1960 as a southbound train approached the structure. The photograph at left illustrates that the bridge was built to accommodate two tracks, but only one track was ever installed. (Both, Chris Thompson collection.)

The IC had several other large bridges in western Kentucky, including across the Tennessee River at Gilbertsville. In the early 1870s, the Elizabethtown and Paducah Railroad erected a drawbridge here. To cut costs, the fixed spans on this bridge were built using heavy wooden beams covered by sheet metal. The photograph above was taken on June 29, 1901. (IC.)

On July 4, 1903, one span of the Gilbertsville bridge caught fire and collapsed. The bridge was out of service until July 8. Railroad officials quickly drafted plans for a new bridge, seen on May 16, 1905, as construction drew to a close. The bridge officially opened for business on July 10. The first train across the bridge was passenger train No. 102, with L. L. "Pop" Cofer at the throttle. (IC.)

In 1938, the Tennessee Valley Authority began construction of a dam across the Tennessee River at Gilbertsville. IC's tracks were rerouted across the bridge. The first train crossed on November 2, 1944, also with L. L. "Pop" Cofer at the throttle. Cofer posed in the cab during brief ceremonies at the dam. This was the last run for Cofer, ending a 61-year career that began in 1883. (IC.)

In its original configuration, the Kentucky Dam carried only railroad tracks. Then, in 1949, construction began on a two-lane highway to carry U.S. Highway 62 and U.S. Highway 641. As seen in mid-1950, construction of the road deck was nearly complete, and soon crews will begin pouring concrete to form the roadway. (Chris Thompson collection.)

Nine

WRECKS AND FLOODS

Railroading has always been a dangerous occupation. During the early 1900s, broken rails, inadequate signal systems, and confusion over train orders lead to numerous derailments and collisions. Many major railroads operated their own hospitals to care for injured and sick employees. One of these hospitals was located at Paducah and was founded in 1884 by Collis P. Huntington, the benevolent president of the CO&SW.

Passengers were not immune from the dangers of the railroads. One of the first recorded rail accidents in western Kentucky occurred on October 11, 1872, when an Elizabethtown and Paducah Railroad passenger train derailed near Paducah, killing two. On October 20, 1912, a broken rail caused an excursion train to derail at Green's Crossing, about 6 miles north of Hopkinsville. There were no fatalities, but 128 passengers were injured.

Mother Nature also made railroading more dangerous. The IC crossed several major rivers in western Kentucky, including the Ohio, Tennessee, Cumberland, and Green Rivers, and passed in close proximity to the "mighty" Mississippi River. Prior to the construction of reservoirs in the 1940s and 1950s, flooding was a problem nearly every year. IC crews became adept at fighting floodwaters.

Nothing could prepare the IC for the colossal flood that hit the Ohio River valley in early 1937. IC's operations were affected all the way from Louisville to Cairo, Illinois. Both the Cairo and Metropolis bridges were impassable for nearly three weeks, affecting train operations all across the IC system.

During the 1937 Ohio River flood, the IC was affected all the way from Louisville south to Cairo, Illinois. This was the scene on February 12 as floodwaters swept across the tracks at milepost 368, approximately 1 mile north of Wickliffe. Not only has the track itself been swept away, but the telegraph poles have been knocked over. (IC.)

Approximately 100 miles of IC track in Kentucky and Illinois were underwater at some point during the flood. On January 26, 1937, workers at Cairo, Illinois, unload U.S. Coast Guard boats from railcars. Boats like these were rushed to the flood zone from cities across the Midwest, South, and as far away as Maine. (IC.)

Thousands of families were forced from their homes during the 1937 flood. Some of these families sought refuge in railroad boxcars. The photographs on pages 121 and 122 were all taken at a temporary "boxcar city" at Ballard Junction near Wickliffe on January 26, 1937. (Chris Thompson collection.)

Many of these boxcars were outfitted with appliances and furniture brought from home. In the center of the photograph is an Old Reliable kitchen stove. Another stove is visible to the left. Stoves were vital equipment because the wooden boxcars of the era were usually quite drafty. (Chris Thompson collection.)

Another family poses in the boxcar they have remodeled as their temporary home. The monotony of living in a boxcar for several weeks is stressful for kids and adults alike, but everyone is smiling. (Chris Thompson collection.)

Not everyone was welcome to stay in the boxcars, including this canine being shoved out the door. During the flood, many people took extraordinary measures to protect their animals. In Paducah, a cow was put on the second-floor balcony of a house on Sixth Street to save it from the floodwaters. A photograph of "Bossie" appeared in the June 1937 issue of *National Geographic*. (Chris Thompson collection.)

This aerial photograph of downtown Cairo, Illinois, was taken at the height of the 1937 flood and illustrates how the city is surrounded by water. The Mississippi River is in the foreground. In the background is the swollen Ohio River, with the flooded Kentucky countryside partially visible in the distance. But thanks to a floodwall built in the early 1900s, most of Cairo stayed dry. (IC.)

During the 1937 flood, several passenger cars were parked at the North Cairo depot. Some of these cars housed flood refugees, while others housed railroad executives sent to the area to oversee the recovery effort. These cars were heated by steam locomotives, in sharp contrast to the boxcars just a few miles away on the other side of the river. (IC.)

123

Train service across the Cairo bridge was suspended on January 27 and did not resume until February 15. The water was still high on February 17 as a northbound passenger train rolled across the bridge. Railroads from Pennsylvania to Illinois transported approximately 200,000 refugees out of the flood zone. (Author's collection.)

Most floodwaters near Wickliffe receded by the time of this February 25 photograph. The track had reopened and trains were running at restricted speeds. But there was much work to be done, including repairing the telegraph and signal poles to the right and picking up tons of debris. (Chris Thompson collection.)

On April 7, 1959, a loaded coal train derailed at McHenry, throwing GP9 numbers 9353 and 9382 off the track. The wrecker from Central City was probably already on the way to the scene when this photograph was taken. Damage to the locomotives was minimal, and both locomotives were quickly returned to service. (Chris Thompson collection.)

On May 1, 1946, a southbound IC train and a northbound GM&O train collided near Wickliffe. The engineer and fireman on the IC train were killed, and GM&O 2-8-2 No. 457 and IC 2-8-2 No. 1203 were extensively damaged. GM&O No. 457 was retired shortly after the wreck, while IC No. 1203 was repaired and remained in service until the late 1950s. (Chris Thompson collection.)

Another notable wreck took place on June 15, 1948, at Rives, Tennessee, about 13 miles south of Fulton on the double-track mainline to Memphis. At approximately 4:00 p.m., freight train Extra No. 1350 North pulled into the center siding at Rives. After the train stopped, the head brakeman uncoupled three cars at the front of the train, including two tankers filled with gasoline. The 2-8-2 No. 1350 pulled back onto the mainline with the three cars in tow. Unaware that the track ahead was occupied, the crew of Extra No. 2351 North plowed into the cars at 35 miles per hour. The gasoline tankers split open, and three employees died in the subsequent inferno, which took several hours to extinguish. The photographs on pages 126 and 127 were taken at the Paducah shops, where the locomotives were sent for repairs. (Both, Sam Harrison collection.)

On page 126, the 4-8-2 No. 2351 is seen being stripped down to the bare boiler. In the top photograph on that page, the smoke box door has been removed, along with the metal jacket around the boiler. Gone too are the drivers, valve gear, and cylinders. In the lower photograph on page 126, the cab has been removed, revealing the back head at the rear of the boiler. The whitish material is asbestos, used to insulate the boiler. Both photographs on this page are of 2-8-2 No. 1350 in storage while awaiting rebuilding. The No. 1350's tender has been uncoupled, providing this rare view (at right) of the rear of the cab. The side view of its cab (below) shows that the boiler jacket had warped from the heat. Despite the severe damage, both locomotives were repaired and returned to service. (Both, Sam Harrison collection.)

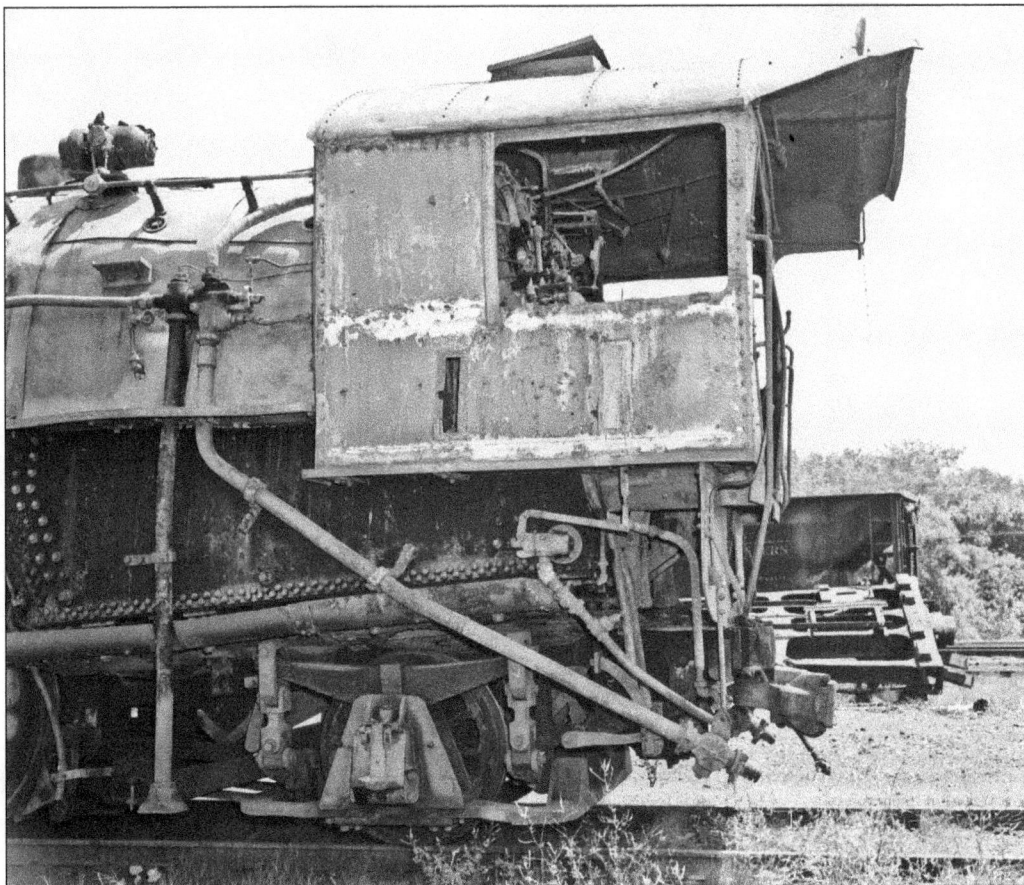

Visit us at
arcadiapublishing.com

www.ingramcontent.com/pod-product-compliance
Lightning Source LLC
Chambersburg PA
CBHW050642110426
42813CB00007B/1891